CW01497602

ANGLO-AMERICAN CAPITALISM AND
THE ETHICS OF
BUSINESS

NORMAN BARRY

NEW ZEALAND BUSINESS ROUNDTABLE
MAY 1999

The New Zealand Business Roundtable is an organisation of chief executives of major New Zealand businesses. The purpose of the organisation is to contribute to the development of sound public policies that reflect overall New Zealand interests.

First published in 1999 by New Zealand Business Roundtable,
PO Box 10–147, The Terrace, Wellington, New Zealand
http://www.nzbr.org.nz

ISBN 1-877148-46-6

© 1999 edition: New Zealand Business Roundtable
© Text: Norman Barry

Design and production by *Daphne Brasell Associates Ltd, Wellington*
Typeset by *Chris Judd*
Printed by *Astra Print Ltd, Wellington*

CONTENTS

PREFACE

This short book marks another stage in the process of trying to understand the nature and philosophy of capitalism. I have been engaged in this process for over 20 years, and despite the victory of market capitalism over communism I have noticed only a small change in the attitudes of intellectuals towards capitalism. The criticism of the market today comes from a different source than from critiques of the past. Marxism is pretty much dead and is preserved only by the remaining professors who were appointed under its aegis. But the new appraisal has an initial plausibility since its upholders often claim some nominal allegiance to the private enterprise market system, although it is preferred if it is the 'social market' or 'communitarian capitalism'.

A large part of the questioning of the theory and practice of market capitalism comes from ethics and religion. To be socially acceptable, business agents need the imprimatur of the moralist or theologian, and the pursuit of profit may only proceed if it satisfies very rigorous moral criteria. The capitalism of Wall Street and the City of London has been picked out as allegedly a particularly venal example of a not morally distinguished economic system. Above all, the market, it is said, cannot generate its own morality, which has to be imposed from outside.

I have been writing and researching these topics for a considerable length of time, and I was particularly pleased to be invited by the New Zealand Business Roundtable to write on them for a New Zealand audience. The pro-market reform programme that began in the 1980s and which soon took New Zealand towards a high position in the league table of free-market societies has been of great interest to me. I wasn't surprised, though, to hear of certain moral criticisms of capitalism made by some writers and economists in New Zealand and so welcomed the opportunity to write a general piece on business ethics which, nevertheless, had some apposite references to the country's experience. New Zealand's economy may be broadly described as 'Anglo-American', but there are enough differences in law and practice to make some important comparisons.

Although my overall aim has been to analyse and appraise Anglo-American capitalism partly by reference to its rivals on the continents of Europe and Asia, there is a fundamental similarity between the different economic philosophies. All the differing types of capitalist systems recognise and depend on a generic morality: it covers trust, honesty, respect for property and the sanctity of contract. These are the basic rules by which we all live, but business and its personnel have been expected to go beyond their narrow confines and take into account the needs of 'society', as well as the rights of shareholders.

I have always wondered why this was so, and writing this book has given me a further opportunity to defend the morality of Anglo-American business against its rivals, whose distinctive features have been sedulously promoted by former socialist intellectuals in the west. The distinctive characteristics of Anglo-American capitalism include its individualism, its search for shareholder value and its encouragement of the takeover method of industrial reorganisation, but these characteristics provoke the most hostility and I have devoted particular attention to them.

A visit to New Zealand in late 1997 alerted me to the minor differences in that country's experience of these issues, and it is my belief that other Anglo-American economies could learn something from New Zealand's variations on a common theme. In the writing of this short book I benefited greatly from many conversations I had on that trip, but I am particularly indebted to Greg Dwyer, Stephen Franks, Michael James, Bernard Robertson and Bryce Wilkinson for their most instructive comments on an earlier draft of this work. They read the document extremely thoroughly and I only hope I have incorporated all of their apposite suggestions and perceptive criticisms. At Buckingham I am grateful to Tanya Franklin for her invaluable editorial assistance during the final stages.

My greatest debt is to Roger Kerr, executive director of the New Zealand Business Roundtable. He introduced me to New Zealand's intellectual experience, to its thriving business culture and to much important written material, all of which I was entirely unaware. These writings were instrumental to the composition of the paper. Most of all, Roger fuelled the project with his perspicacity and inspiring enthusiasm for intellectual arguments about the free market and the nature of liberal society.

Norman Barry

EXECUTIVE SUMMARY

In the wake of the collapse of communism and socialism, including many modern experiments in collectivism and welfarism such as those of New Zealand, critics have produced new appraisals of capitalism and the market. Although many of the critics accept the efficiency of the market, they now subject it to different sorts of tests; tests that are derived mainly from ethics, but also from religion and social philosophy in general. Business people have regularly observed the moral conventions of everyday life – honesty, promise-keeping, respect for justly acquired property and special concern for family and friends – not because they are more virtuous than anyone else but because the practice of commerce encourages the preservation of basic moral standards. However, a special sort of business ethics has emerged from the new appraisals of the free market. Critics expect business personnel to measure up to criteria beyond this ordinary morality: to act for the community even when this involves a sacrifice of profit, to promote equality in the workplace, to take special care of the environment and to satisfy many other prescriptions of supererogatory (or non-compulsory) ethics. Business personnel are perceived to be privileged and therefore owe something to society in return for their advantages.

The critics of the free market analyse different forms of capitalism in accordance with the wider moral criteria of the new business ethics. The critics find that Anglo-American capitalism (practised in America, Britain and much of the English-speaking world, including New Zealand), with its apparently excessive individualism and exclusive concern for profit, is particularly condemnable. Other market economies, especially those of Germany and Japan, are praised because their participants are said to show more concern for the community and for employment, and less for shareholders. European and Asian market economies are seen as less anonymous, they provide opportunities for the exercise of social virtues such as equality and social justice, and greed is apparently less a feature of commerce. These economies are less concerned about the value of private property and, especially in Japan, a strict application of the rule of law.

The public corporation is a particular target of the critics of capitalism. Critics consider that the right of corporations to entity status, to sue and, especially, to limited liability for debt and for torts are privileges. Because of these perceived advantages, the corporation is expected to act often in a non-profit way by promoting ends such as welfare for its employees and special environmental protection – activities that fall more appropriately in the province of law and government. However, historically, these alleged privileges emerged through contracting under private law. In theory, the corporation possesses no more rights than its individual members. The managements of corporations are under strict fiduciary duties to advance the interests of the owners (normally shareholders). However, they often like to practise an alternative form of business ethics as it sometimes relieves them of these fiduciary duties.

The theory of stakeholder-controlled corporations – a part of the new business ethics – subverts complex property and contractual relationships. Proponents of this theory argue that because stakeholders (who are not normally shareholders) are closely connected to the corporation, as employees or residents of the area in which the company is situated, they should have decision rights over such matters as wages and the location of plant. However, there is no one body of stakeholders with a coherent voice; they are, in reality, sectional and competing groups who seek extra-market privileges from the corporation. Few people would invest in a fully-fledged stakeholder company because in it ownership and shareholder rights are seriously attenuated.

The new criticisms of Anglo-American capitalism also target the stock market, not only because large profits can be made there, but also because it is said to create opportunities for fraud and deception. The most contentious feature of the stock market is insider dealing. This is thought to be an especially egregious offence because it apparently involves a serious breach of fiduciary duty on the part of employees of a company who trade in its stocks with advance information. Insider dealing also unfairly disadvantages other external shareholders. However, it is unclear whether the company itself owns all the value that it creates. Entrepreneurship does take place within the firm and perhaps its creators should be entitled to some of the profits (beyond normal salary). Very strict enforcement of insider dealing regulations is a threat to the rule of law since the difficulty of precisely defining the offence means the law is unpredictable. This is especially important when insider dealing is criminalised. A solution to the problem would be to make permission to trade in the company's shares a matter of contract with its employees, enforceable at private law. New Zealand has the merit of leaving it to private individuals to bring legal actions and, although the conditions for the civil offence are similar to those in the more rigorous legal regimes of America and Britain, the law in New Zealand does not seem to be a great deterrent to stock market operations.

Anglo-American capitalism is distinguished from other forms of capitalism by its use of the takeover method of industrial reorganisation. Critics say that the takeover process is only necessary to discipline management because the system itself is characterised by lack of trust. Some of the most notorious business scandals of the 1980s, including insider dealing, occurred during takeover battles, and the use by managements of controversial tactics, such as 'greenmail' and the 'poison pill', was especially condemnable. However, the right to sell one's shares to the highest bidder is an essential feature of economic liberty and the exercise of this right has generated great flexibility and adaptability in Anglo-American capitalism. There is no uncontroversial concept of the 'common good' that can be used to validate excessive restrictions on individualistic takeovers. In fact, most of the immorality associated with this technique stems from managements using unacceptable methods, involving a breach of duty to their shareholders, to resist corporate raiders. New Zealand is similar to other Anglo-American economies, but the concentrated ownership here of listed companies has led to the fear that small shareholders might be exploited in a takeover, and there is a demand in New Zealand that all shareholders be treated the same (which is obligatory in the British Takeover Code). The case for mandatory equal treatment has not been satisfactorily made, but under the Stock Exchange's listing rules there is now a shareholder choice of three different takeover regimes, one of which includes equal treatment.

Anglo-American capitalism has been accused of despoiling the environment and unnecessarily depleting scarce natural resources in its search for profit. Some environmental activists are against human progress and are prepared to value nature and the animal world above the needs of human beings. They advance intervention and regulation by the state – yet there is no evidence that the state has a good record in environmental preservation. The sensible environmental debate is based on economic rather than ethical principles, although the debate must also take into account 'public good' problems since no one rational economic agent has any incentive to preserve goods which are consumed by everyone. The solution to environmental problems is a clear definition of property rights so that the victims of damage can sue the perpetrators. The critics' fear that scarce resources will, under the free market, become exhausted is erroneous: in fact the prices of the major commodities have fallen over the last decade.

It is not true that all business scandals in Anglo-American economies are particularly venal. Because of their strong commitment to the rule of law, openness to newcomers and ordered competitiveness, these economies have avoided the corruption and 'cronyism' that have featured in Asian communitarian capitalist economies. One of the great cultural achievements of Anglo-American capitalism is that it generates honesty between transactors who do not know one another; it does not require the intimacy, and therefore avoids the prejudices, of communal arrangements.

I
THE RISE OF
BUSINESS ETHICS

The market economy, capitalism and the business culture in general are now undergoing what is perhaps their most searching enquiry in the post-war period. Capitalism, since its beginning, has been subject to intense scrutiny, especially from the intellectual class in western liberal democracies. This group of people seems destined to be permanently alienated from that system of production and exchange which is not only the source of great prosperity, but is also the model emulated by countries less favoured by history and circumstances than the United States, the English-speaking world in general and Western Europe. However, the critical examination of capitalism is a little different from that of the past. Against traditional Marxist attacks, capitalism's defenders usually engaged in grand arguments in history, sociology, philosophy, political economy and the general social sciences. Although the opponents of capitalism never doubted its iniquity, they were much more concerned with demonstrating its inevitable decline, according to irresistible historical laws, than with exposing some nefarious stock market scandal or particularly egregious example of corporate misbehaviour. Indeed, the traditional Marxists were reluctant to condemn capitalism by the criteria of western morality since they doubted the intellectual credibility of that ethics anyway.

However, the collapse of communist central planning and the manifest failure of more modest socialist experiments, such as those of New Zealand[1] and Scandinavia, have brought a renewed interest in the theory of capitalist free-market economics and, not surprisingly, fresh sources of criticism from erstwhile adherents of state direction and control. The anti-capitalist rhetoric has been no less fierce than before but has a new plausibility precisely because it emanates from sources that are nominally predisposed towards market capitalism. Important among these sources is the business ethics movement,[2] a trend of opinion that does not aim at the overthrow of capitalism but seeks to validate it (or condemn it) by reference to a morality which is *external* to it, that is, one that is not specifically related to the practice of business but has more to do with the promotion of wider social ideals. Free exchange conducted according to the rule of law between consenting adults is, by itself, insufficient to guarantee the acceptability of the enterprise society. Instead free exchange must be subject to the whole panoply of western ethical and political philosophy and evaluated by reference to social justice, communitarianism, positive liberty and other substantive social concepts which have little to do with business enterprise and which are, as we shall show, inimical to it. It would seem that these 'friendly' critics of capitalism are not so much concerned with appraising contemporary capitalism as a total economic system but with subjecting particular aspects of it, such as the alleged power and irresponsibility of the corporation, the lack of social concern shown by the corporate raider and the unconscionable greed of the stock market investor, to relentless criticism. The aim of business ethics seems not to be to demolish capitalism (at least not directly) but to sanitise it with some heavy philosophical detergents. The business agent these days is a bit like someone unfortunate enough to face an audit from the tax authorities – every feature of their activity and every payment received, no matter how small, has to be explained and justified. All of this may lack the glamour of the great ideological debates of the past but it is irksome nonetheless.

The business ethics movement has distinguished various forms of capitalism in accordance with their moral grading, as measured by enlightened moral and social philosophy. Hence Anglo-American capitalism, the system practised on Wall Street, the City of London and the English-speaking world in general, scores rather lowly with such business ethics moralists because of its perceived remorseless individualism and exclusive profit motivation. Japanese, Asian and certain types of European market economies, however, are praised because in them greed and self-interest are said to be restrained by morals of a more communitarian origin. Some of these restraints are combined with efficiency considerations. Thus the self-interested motivations that drive the takeover process of a company are said to be not only morally condemnable, in that they leave valuable social groups and long-established and integrative industrial arrangements to the mercy of the market, but they encourage 'short-termism' to the detriment of economically valuable projects which are not rated highly by the ephemeral and transient verdict of the stock market. Business moralists make much of the fact that two of the most successful capitalist economies, Japan and Germany, show a marked distaste for the takeover mechanism; this hostility is as much a consequence of a shared social distrust of financiers as it is of legal prohibitions. The current rethinking of the ethics of capitalism is partially inspired by the experience of rivals of the Anglo-American model, although events in the past four or five years have added considerable credence to both the efficiency and ethics of that system. Too many of the critics of Anglo-American capitalism are ill-informed about the workings of the system and are sublimely ignorant of both the economic and moral failings of its rivals.

New Zealand fits easily into the Anglo-American model of capitalism; most of the country's economic practices and institutions, such as the financing of companies through the stock market and the prevalence of profit-motivated individual entrepreneurship, are a direct product of a common colonial heritage which the present-day inhabitants (anti-capitalist intellectuals excepted) show little intention of altering. Just as writers in the United States and Britain have shown an increasing critical awareness of the alleged moral deficiencies of Anglo-American capitalism, similar thoughts are also expressed in New Zealand. The business ethics movement has been given added force in New Zealand because of the country's remarkable success in enacting free-market reforms in the past 15 years. After decades of national sloth in a semi-socialist, welfarist and regulatory environment, the entrepreneurial skills of New Zealand's people have been released into a new environment of less intrusive government, freer trade and fewer direct governmental controls on working practices and output. The skills and aptitudes are quite conventional but had been rendered dormant in New Zealand by years of excessive governmental regulation.

New Zealand has recently been ranked third in a world league table for its level of economic freedom.[3] Such a 'revolution' in economic practice has naturally provoked considerable opposition and much of this has had an ethical inspiration. Allegedly, New Zealand's historic reputation for honesty, probity, fair dealing, trust and compassion has been compromised in the rush towards markets and individualism. Some of these criticisms seem in fact to be quite gratuitous since, by any established and respected moral grading agency, New Zealand is characterised by a remarkable honesty and probity both in its business and political life.[4] If business morality is interpreted as the 'thou shalt nots' of Christian and other religious doctrines, New Zealand business people are solicitous in their protection of property rights and in the honouring of contracts. New Zealand has experienced few of the business scandals that have occurred in the City of London and on Wall Street and, though the incidence of the latter has been much exaggerated, such scandals illustrate the temptations to which those engaged in commerce are peculiarly susceptible.

The most striking feature of recent business ethics is the emphasis not merely on the basic duties of refraining from action that violates the rights of others but on the newer, and much more controversial and contestable, duties to provide positive goods outside the price mechanism. In the language of technical moral philosophy, these are called *supererogatory* duties, that is, desirable but not compelling. It would be morally worthy if someone were to devote 20 percent of their income to charity, but the failure to do so would not be thought of as morally condemnable. On the other hand, the obligation to refrain from cheating and lying is strictly compelling and we would not be expected to earn much moral credit from observing these rules of justice. Business ethics has tried to present supererogatory duties as if they were obligations of a strictly compelling kind. For example, the New Zealand businessman Dick Hubbard has argued that businesses should donate 10 percent of their profits to worthy causes.[5] Of course, it is highly unlikely that this will become a duty of the positive law (and if it were to become so, its observance would hardly be counted as a genuine moral act) but the proponents of this ethical strategy clearly wish to extend the range of what might be called enforceable virtue – so that charity becomes as morally compelling as justice.

It is noticeable that ordinary human agents are not expected to perform supererogatory duties, at least not in the normal course of events. Why then should business personnel be subjected to these more demanding moral standards? The argument would seem to be that business activity operates in a position of privilege and that its personnel owe something back to society in return for these advantages – there is a kind of moral licence to operate which must be earned. The alleged advantages of the corporate form is the favourite example of this privilege, and on this is built the heady list of social duties which companies are supposed to fulfil. But even in the absence of these alleged privileges, business still has to validate its right to make profits. Perhaps the success of an enterprise depends on its ability to exploit 'informational asymmetries' (relative ignorance of consumers in comparison to the knowledge of unscrupulous producers); business might enjoy a monopolistic position (or some other market imperfection) which makes its profits 'unjust'; or its position in the employment market may generate coercive power over defenceless workers. All of these aberrations from morality must be explained, justified and probably eliminated.

Factors such as business and employment market monopoly have been used by business ethicists to bolster their claim that commerce cannot be validated by conventional morality. Perhaps, like the medical and legal professions, commerce requires some special tribunal to investigate its wrongdoings. It is, however, difficult to see how commerce can be counted as a profession, of which the breach of professional rules could be properly justiciable. Commerce does have certain practices and conventions on the observance of which its success depends.

BUSINESS, SELF-INTEREST AND RELIGION

The most important single fact, which has led to the attempted moralisation of business, is the all-pervading presence of self-interest as its major motivating force. Too many people are embarrassed by the fact that the desire to better ourselves is a feature of almost all human activity, and they assuage their moral guilt by concentrating their fire on the activity that seems to depend exclusively on the baser instincts (unlike professions, such as law and medicine, whose spokespeople seek some validation in the claim that their *raison d'etre* is the promotion of the public interest, no matter how implausible that may be in some cases). Christianity has undoubtedly had much to do with the campaign to impose impossibly high standards on business, and to the propagation of its alleged morally tainted biography. By stressing the importance of business's main motivation, some Christian spokespeople have managed to deflect attention away from the tremendous achievements of the private enterprise market economy in providing consumer goods, high employment and considerable personal freedom. In Adam Smith's famous words: "It is not from the benevolence of the butcher, baker and brewer that we get our dinner but from their regard to their self-interest".[6] The success, then, of business is largely a function of its suspension of the altruistic motivation. It is not only the encouragement of the qualified egoistic motivation that is relevant here. Also important is the claim of market economics that social well-being is not a result of artifice and design but is the almost accidental outcome of many individual actions, none of which was aimed at the public good. The contemporary Christian doubt about the morality of business enterprise stems partly from the latter's dependence on the baser motives of egoism and self-interest and partly from the belief that only social activism can bring about virtue, a moral conceit that has become such a feature of *politicised* modern religion.

Yet doubt did not always exist. The foundations of the modern market economy were laid down in the Catholic religion by the theoretical enquiries of the School of Salamanca in sixteenth-century Spain.[7] What is relevant to modern business ethics is that the 'just price' was never an idealised, heavily moralistic notion of the value of goods abstracted from their commercial worth, but simply the statement that goods should exchange at prices uninfluenced by monopolistic practices. Again, at this time, there was no theory of wages deriving from social justice; factor earnings simply reflected the verdict of the labour market. Historically the major religions have not evinced a disdain for commerce. Early Protestantism was associated with the rise of capitalism and Islam[8] has from its beginning encouraged entrepreneurship – indeed Khaldun hit upon the theory of the market economy even before the Catholics at Salamanca.

With the exception of Judaism, the religious doctrines have had some difficulty with monetary interest, or the Riba in Islamic doctrine, which is an essential feature of capitalistic development. Enquiries have shown that religious doctrines have not decreed a blanket ban on the charging of interest on monetary loans; the limitations placed on loans normally apply to particularly egregious and exploitative interest charges and the moral principle invoked is of the negative kind – 'Thou shalt not exploit the weak and vulnerable'. Traditional religious doctrine does not impose heavy social duties on business agents or require them to abstain from normal utility-maximising behaviour; the market economy was seen as part of the 'natural world', and condemnation was reserved for those actions that were in breach of 'natural law', that is, the morality that governs all human relationships, including economic ones, and which precedes positive law.

Modern religious doctrine, however, is much more likely to stress the supererogatory virtues and tends to go along with the doctrine that says that business, because it depends on self-interest, must express contrition at this moral failing by doing positive good for the public. There was a welcome departure from this approach with Pope John Paul's encyclical, *Centesimus Annus* (1991), which resuscitated the original Catholic approval of commerce.[9] In it entrepreneurship is recognised and encouraged, and there is little of the heavy moralising against commerce and the profit motive which had characterised Papal documents since Pope Leo XIII's encyclical *Rerum Novarum* (1891).

Part of the Christian moral scepticism toward markets and capitalism derives from 'conventional' values borrowed from some contemporary doctrines of social science and political economy. Much of the conventional wisdom in these areas is misleading. Thus although the economics profession, unlike other branches of the social sciences, has not been uniformly opposed to markets, private property and the price mechanism, it has tended to interpret these phenomena in overly critical ways. Even believers in markets tend to look sedulously for examples of market failure, where, for technical reasons, the price system does not produce 'public' goods (wanted goods that cannot be priced and supplied by the market).[10] The range of public goods has been extended way beyond the familiar ones of defence, clean air and law and order to include education, welfare and health care. This has had a deleterious effect on business, especially in areas such as the environment where it is automatically assumed that business alone is responsible for the depredations that have occurred.

These criticisms have all occurred at a time when technological progress has actually narrowed the range of public goods. Such is the lure of substantive equality that certain seductive arguments from orthodox economics have been borrowed and made serviceable for moral ends. Thus perfect competition (a theoretical state of affairs in which all entrepreneurial profits have been competed away, and price equals long-run marginal costs of production) has been presented as the ideal economic world. In such an unlikely nirvana, business ethics would hardly be needed since all the circumstances, for example monopoly and asymmetric information, that generate moral problems would have been defined away. There would be no problem of insider dealing on the stock market since in this world all participants possess perfect knowledge of all possible states of affairs, and power in the workplace would be absent since each 'employee' could instantaneously contract their way out of a less than propitious working environment.

However, we do not live in a world of perfect competition and there are consequently opportunities for excess 'profit', and many occasions on which astute individuals can take advantage of especially favourable positions in the market place, such as securing quasi-monopolies, and employers can acquire dominance and power over workers. The latter can occur not only in times of unemployment but also when employees invest their human capital in a particular occupation with little transfer value; such 'firm-specific' labour becomes particularly vulnerable in the event of a takeover. It is phenomena such as these that lead to the demand that business behave in a socially responsible manner, to perform supererogatory duties, to display 'corporate citizenship' and forgo profit in order to satisfy allegedly pressing moral demands. If we add contemporary concerns over the environment and the demands of an ever-expanding list of rights, we find that business is gradually burdened with social duties that go way beyond the obligations of ordinary citizens. It is here that religion and a heavily moralistic intellectual opinion have together posed serious threats to the viability of capitalism, while simultaneously critics have paid obeisance (albeit nominally) to the market system. The fact that such critiques are made in anodyne terms is another reason for pro-capitalist thinkers and spokespersons to be on their guard.

WHAT ETHICS FOR BUSINESS?

To cast doubt on the relevance of a supererogatory morality for business and to recognise the necessity, indeed the social value, of self-interest is not to jettison ethics from commerce nor to accept its amorality. It is true that there is a tradition, dating back to the eighteenth century, which suggests that there is a dichotomy between virtue and commerce, that success in business does necessitate a suspension of our normal morals. It is a view that found expression in successful recent Hollywood movies, for example, *Wall Street, Other People's Money* and *Pretty Woman*, that satirised the 1980s as the 'decade of greed' and condemned business agents as purveyors of a certain kind of amorality.

This view has a certain intellectual pedigree that begins with Bernard Mandeville's comic poem *The Fable of the Bees* (first published in 1705). In his notorious parable Mandeville portrayed the bees in the beehive as greedy, selfish and indifferent to popular morality. But in this 'happy state' the division of labour, the market, free trade and overall prosperity were developed from the actions of self-seeking individuals who had no moral sense at all ("Each part was full of vice/But the whole a paradise"[11]). In a later accompanying essay he said that: "The grand principle that makes us social creatures, the solid basis, the life and support of all trade, without exception is evil".[12] However, once the bees 'got morality' they became fractious, quarrelsome and impoverished. Mandeville was saying that to achieve economic success, people must be liberated from conventional constraints; he thought that morality was hypocrisy anyway, and that ethics were mere contrivances to keep people in order. It is a view which today finds *sotto voce* support from some business agents and renegade 'moralists'. Self-interest is a position which Adam Smith tried hard to refute, while, at the same time, retaining some of its economically useful tenets. A modern example of Mandevillianism was given by the arbitrager (and convicted insider dealer) Ivan Boesky, who once said in a famous speech to business students: "Greed is all right ... I want you to know that. I think greed is healthy. You can be greedy and still feel good about yourself".[13]

There is no doubt that Mandeville had hit upon some of the key features of commerce, but his wholesale dismissal of morality is misleading and dangerous to business itself. To start with, his definition of morality is extremely narrow, even eccentric. He seems to be saying that morality consists exclusively of self-sacrifice, that the true moral agent is anxious to suppress all motivations of self-interest on behalf of a dubious notion of the common good. He has little difficulty in showing that this is an impossible demand to make of individuals; if they did not behave selfishly in business they would express their greed in politics or in some other less socially useful human activity.

In a curious way, Mandeville and his epigones are reflecting the ethics of the modern business activist who would impose positive social duties on the modern enterprise; both regard business as immoral. The only and obvious difference is that the Mandevillian would regard such duties as undesirable, indeed impossible – we have to accept immorality if we are to be commercially successful. Similarly, the moralists argue that business is basically unethical and only if it changes its nature is it to be permitted.

But morality is by no means exclusively concerned with overt self-sacrifice, altruism or displays of public virtue. These features are a small part of what we normally mean by ethical conduct and are the aspects less likely to flourish in the business world, however appropriate they might be in family and other close personal relationships. Conventional moral behaviour is exhibited by following of the rules of just conduct, by respecting legitimately acquired property and in honouring contracts.

What is more disturbing about the Mandevillian view of ethics is that the description of human nature which it uses makes it very difficult for us to understand how rules essential to business enterprise could ever be viable. For commercial activity does require a certain amount of self-restraint. In some areas, especially finance and, increasingly, the environment, the business community advances its own interests when it observes certain rules, which it does normally. This not only serves to ward off undesirable and profit-reducing government regulation, it also helps business to run more smoothly. Specifically, when business agents develop trust it cuts down on transaction costs. Business personnel rely on partners to keep their word and to honour agreements voluntarily, and these cooperative actions reduce the reliance by business personnel on lawyers. One of the valid criticisms of American commerce is that it requires heavy outlays in legal costs. It is true that America is a high trust society in general,[14] but it is also the case that it needs a lot more lawyers to make business work effectively than appears to be the case in more communitarian commercial orders. As we shall see later, much of the criticism here has been exaggerated and communitarian capitalism has disadvantages of its own, yet it is still true that business does better when it develops habits of self-restraint. But the occasional lurid scandal should not be used to denigrate business as a whole.

The cultivation and observance of rules of restraint is the only way in which it can be plausibly said that 'business ethics pays'. These rules might very well be thought of more as a form of prudence than genuine morality since they contribute to overall well-being or profitability, but they are still clearly different from Mandevillian egoism because they require people to follow a rule even when it would be in their short-run advantage to break it. This breaking of such rules might well harm the business community overall, even though the individual might profit from such immorality. Indeed, the business community itself might turn out to be an effective policing agency for the enforcement of rules. However, the significant point about business enterprise, and its associated morality, is that it develops through a continuous process of exchange between self-interested parties who have every incentive to cooperate. David Hume, the eighteenth-century philosopher and early expositor of the market, described the trading relationship between two farmers in terms that are still appropriate today. He wrote:

> Your corn is ripe today; mine will be ripe tomorrow. Tis profitable for us both, that I should labour with you today, and that you should aid me tomorrow. I have no kindness to you, and know you have as little for me ... . Hence I learn to do a service to another, without bearing any real kindness, because I foresee that he returns my service.[15]

The key concept for the business relationship that is described here is *reciprocity*, an attribute which does not depend on benevolence but derives from sophisticated self-interest. Individuals do better if they learn to treat each other as equals entitled to respect. This is not a function of their being members of identifiable groups united by religion, race or culture but by being potential partners in the pursuit of monetary gain, from which society as a whole benefits in a utilitarian sense. It was a human capacity that allowed commercial law to develop from medieval times and that was the feature of the early London Stock Exchange, well described by Voltaire on a visit to England.[16] He noticed that it was a venue in which people of a variety of religions could deal with each other in security – its rules were self-enforcing. It is a mistake of modern business ethics to concentrate only on the business scandals and to ignore the myriad of examples of business coordination through abstract rules. The ethics of Anglo-American business are essentially those of individualists who have a common interest in reinforcing the rules of enterprise through repeated plays of the game. This is why standards of ethics rise with the greater penetration of society by the principles of the free enterprise system. Individuals see the value of coordinating their activities by observing common rules. This contrasts remarkably with communist systems in which corruption, bribery and cheating were often the only ways in which anything could be done or produced. Less extreme forms of socialism do not produce high standards of morality.

In a clear contrast to modern business ethics, the morality of Anglo-American commerce is intrinsic to the activity itself. Yet it is a feature of almost all contemporary business moralists that they persist in claiming that commercial morality and its rules somehow have to be imposed from non-market sources. This is true even of writers favourable to the capitalist market system. The prominent post-war German market theorist, Wilhelm Röpke, wrote that "the market, competition and the play of supply and demand do not create ethical reserves; they presuppose and consume them. These ethical reserves must come from *outside* the market".[17] But from where do they come? The state, moral philosophy, religion? It is quite likely that they will emanate from sources not excessively favourable to the market. When we say that the market generates its own rules of conduct, that is not meant to imply that it is completely self-sufficient: after all, the market depends to an extent on rules against theft, violence and so forth, and these rules have their origin in general, social relationships. However, market rules do not come from outside the whole nexus of social interactions; they are not extrinsic to them but emerge without design from within them. They become so accepted through repeated interaction that, as Hume recognised, they acquire a moral gloss apart from their convenience as conventions. This makes obedience much easier to enforce.

The post-war German market system was fairly quickly transformed into the social market economy (with the accent on the social), and eventually degenerated into social democracy. It was not a movement of ideas that was confined to the political arena but also affected business itself; hence the cultural hostility to takeovers and the reluctance of business to embrace the goal of increasing shareholder value.

It is imperative to point out that the rules of Anglo-American business are properly universal and make no distinctions between traders on merely contingent factors such as religion, race or national origin. Those who criticise this form of capitalism from the standpoint of communitarian capitalism or the much-admired systems of Japan and Asia should be aware of the fact that these systems are very much enclosed commercial orders that, for all their virtues, erect informal barriers to entry and operate through complex informal rule structures (such as the *Keiretsu* in Japan). These structures conceal what would be considered quite immoral practices by the more open commercial and moral principles of Anglo-American business.[18]

Anonymity is the one feature of the Hume model of commercial ethics that might, superficially, make it less applicable to the modern world than it was to the scarcely developed business world of the eighteenth century, with its small proprietors and closely knit communities. In contrast to earlier practice, part of modern business is relatively anonymous. Traders tend to meet as strangers and in international finance they scarcely meet at all, except via a computer screen. This anonymity might be thought to inhibit the development of self-enforcing rules of commerce, but its effect can be exaggerated. These rules have developed over a long period of time and new recruits to business are inducted, almost unwittingly, into established business practices. It is unlikely that strangers, who perhaps meet rarely, would overnight 'create' just rules, but this is not often required. What is essential to modern business is the internalisation of those rules that have proved their usefulness to commerce through a process of evolution. Repeated plays of the business game eventually eliminate non-cooperators.

Hume's great friend, Adam Smith, famously argued that collaboration between merchants would inevitably lead to conspiracies against the consumer. Smith was also deeply suspicious, for efficiency reasons, of the joint stock company, fearing that only owner-managers would have an interest in maximising the value of assets. The first complaint, of collaboration between merchants, is a common one and is not without justification, but it ignores the prophylactic effect of the market and competition. All human agents have a propensity to combine for bad, as well as good, reasons. But Smith, the apostle of the market, seemed reluctant to recognise its beneficial consequences in less than propitious circumstances. Business combinations are more fragile the more open and competitive the market is. The most harmful effects of business combinations are felt when they pressurise governments to introduce market-closing interventions, especially protectionism, and it is here that commerce is worthy of the severest moral censure. Competition is in the public interest but no one particular person has an immediate incentive to promote it.

As for Smith's problem with the joint stock company, the solution in Anglo-American capitalism is to develop the market for corporate control (the takeover mechanism). All managements are prone to maximise their own interests rather than those of the shareholders, and the only remedy shareholders have is to sell their stock to someone who promises to manage the assets more efficiently. In the relatively anonymous world of Anglo-American business it is a potent method of ensuring good management performance. However, the takeover method has been particularly criticised by business ethicists for its alleged greed, insouciance with regard to community values and indifference to the welfare of loyal employees.

INSOLUBLE PROBLEMS?

Although the kind of business ethics outlined above, with its stress on the importance of self-regulation and on the relevance to conduct of informal, minimalist rules, is extremely effective in most circumstances, it comes up against a familiar problem in social theory – the 'public good trap'.[19] This 'public good trap' has been much exaggerated but it does pose problems for any social doctrine that wishes to reduce the role of the state, for either moral or efficiency reasons. In some activities, rational self-interest may produce outcomes unwelcome to the business agents themselves. It is in the self-interest of each citizen that we have defence and law and order, that there is clean air and other things that are consumed collectively, but it is not in the interests of separate individuals to promote these things since they cannot be sure that others will be cooperative and contribute voluntarily to the production of the wanted good, or refrain from the harmful activity.

There is, therefore, a role for the state to prevent 'free riding' on the goodwill of others (which, in the circumstances, will be short lived). In the business world it is clearly exhibited in the problem of pollution (a 'negative externality'). Although voluntary cooperation could solve common problems through repeated plays of the game (in order to identify non-cooperators quickly and eliminate them through an evolutionary process) cooperation is less likely to happen over pollution. Damage to the environment is caused not by the external effects of all industrial development (most business activity generates some), but by the *additional* polluter who makes things intolerable. The additional polluter cannot easily be identified and made the subject of legal or (appropriate) social action – it has made its profit and disappeared, leaving others worse off. The result of this situation is that the state takes action through positive law, which normally operates through blanket bans and restrictions.

It is likely that if businesses had been more cooperative in the United States there would not be the need now for the excessive compliance costs imposed on businesses by successive clean air and clean water acts. The pollution is not caused by the immorality of business people but by the perverse incentive structure that each company faces. In such circumstances it is rather pointless of business ethics to attempt to moralise business agents. Nevertheless, there have been a number of attempts to get around the pollution problem by market methods, all of which centre on the need for more appropriate property rights. This is one area that requires an extraordinary amount of cooperation by private business personnel if over-regulation is to be avoided. The relative anonymity of a modern market economy makes fruitful business cooperation and self-regulation difficult.

Still, we should not despair of business agents cooperating for their own advantage, for the problems they face are not always like the classic 'prisoners dilemmas' of social theory. In these dilemmas a game is played only once and each player has an incentive to defect from an agreement since they cannot rely on the other player(s). The political philosopher, Thomas Hobbes, attempted to demonstrate the need for an absolute sovereign in precisely these conditions. In the business world, however, trade tends to be a continuing process and this allows trust to be built between parties. There is a harmony between morality and efficiency. This is known as the 'iterated prisoners dilemma' in game theory: repetition allows trust to develop. Of course, the players are in a good position to identify and punish defectors.

There are other business issues which involve similar problems, notably in financial markets, and these are discussed later in detail. It should be stressed at this point that the problems of business ethics should be accommodated within the familiar structure of conventional western morality. The rules of this structure are simple to grasp and internalise, and their observance does not involve the threats to efficiency and prosperity that observance of an over-expansive business ethics does, anxious as it is to impose supererogatory duties on business. These duties are certain to be prosperity-reducing and a threat to the property rights of all participants.

The contents of the type of ethics that should restrain business agents should include the common rules of society that apply to all citizens. These rules are consistent with the prescriptions of traditional religions which are basically elaborations of the fundamental 'do nots' of civil society. The assumption by a business of supererogatory duties, either voluntarily or through moral pressure, and legislated business ethics are likely to have serious implications for the role of commerce in providing employment and cheap and reliable goods and services. But a description of these rules is not uncomplicated and may reveal indeterminacies and potential conflicts. One obvious conflict is that between the demands of consequentialism or utility, that is, the maximisation of individual satisfactions, conveniently (but not quite accurately) measured in terms of disposable incomes, and deontological rules that restrain action irrespective of consequences.[20] The deontological rules include procedural justice; some actions are felt not to be right even if they do generate beneficial consequences. It is for a good reason that the rules of the Paris Bourse are called 'Les Principes des Déontologies'.

However, this notion of procedural justice should not be confused with social justice or some ideal distribution of income and wealth, about which there is unlikely to be agreement. It is not the responsibility of the managers of businesses to determine wages so as to bring about such a distribution of income and wealth; they cannot do so without abrogating the rights of the business owners. Managers are, however, under a strict duty to honour contracts. When modern business is burdened with additional moral responsibilities (the supererogatory duties) the fundamental property rights structure is threatened. Those who make such claims, especially in fashionable areas such as the environment, are indulging in a certain kind of moral vanity – whether they are professional philosophers, members of the clergy or morally inspired company executives who act in a non-profit maximising way. The actions of these business agents involve no cost to themselves. However, a proper supererogatory ethics must involve a cost to the actor. The moralistic executive is in quite a different position from, say, the private owner who does forgo income for what they think is a justified cause. When this morality is expected to be provided by the corporation it becomes something of a consumer good supplied by other people, normally the shareholders. Those who benefit from the esteem it gives them do not pay the full costs.

The relevance of all these considerations is more clearly seen in the analysis in the next chapter of the major institutions and policies of the modern business world.

2
THE CORPORATION

Business ethics has focused attention on the corporation, and the practice of converting supererogatory moral actions into duties of a compelling kind has been carried out most thoroughly and controversially in the case of the ethics of corporate life. Whenever the theory of the social responsibility of the corporation is discussed, it often means that the owners and managers of this form of capitalist organisation are to be subject to critical censure that would not be applied to non-corporate citizens, or even to the members of other professions, such as medicine or law. Managers are to be persuaded or compelled to act in a way which is inconsistent with their primary obligation of providing returns to shareholders, and, even where their moral duties are confined to the ordinary 'do nots' of morality, the conditions for their legal responsibility have toughened in recent years. For example, the corporation can be treated as a real, biological person for the purposes of the criminal law, and although the process has gone further in America, where corporations have been convicted of serious criminal offences, than in Britain or elsewhere in the English-speaking world, the indications are that popular hostility against the corporation may be translated into legal coercion.[21]

The traditional collectivist hostility towards the corporation is undoubtedly derived from the general moral criticism of capitalism. It is argued by the critics of capitalism that the freedom for the individual celebrated by market theorists was illusory because the form in which capitalism had developed (or mutated) negates any advancement of liberty that its apologists might claim. The market system under liberal capitalism, it is said, does not protect liberty because it is dominated by corporations that are immune from the competitive forces of the price system and the corrective power of the liberal state. J K Galbraith, for example, thought it was useless to try to moralise the corporation, as business ethics has attempted, since its internal mechanisms were somehow exempt from any kind of regulation. It could only be checked by a 'countervailing power'.[22] What has made the corporation particularly powerful is the growth of international trade and the increased mobility of capital; this growth and increased mobility has enabled international corporations to move to countries and states with the most favourable laws. These corporations therefore can easily flee the tough environmental and labour protection laws of the west and continue to pollute the environment and to treat workers badly in poorer countries that need employment more than they need a clean atmosphere and pleasant working conditions.

Even within the doctrine of capitalism the justification for the corporation has proved to be difficult to assert. Its collective form, implicit power relations within its personnel structure and 'plan-like' behaviour seem redolent of socialist control rather than free markets. Even sympathetic commentators have remarked on its quasi-coercive features. Sir Denis Robertson and Stanley Dennison noticed that it generated "islands of conscious power in an ocean of unconscious cooperation".[23] What they had in mind was a contrast between catallactics, the pure exchange between individuals who are free to transact with whomever they choose, and modern business with its complex system of *bilateral* contracting. Under the latter, the employee is tied to the corporation and must obey the commands of a superior: it is a 'master-servant' relationship, rather than one of market freedom. However, the modern corporation developed spontaneously, and employees are always free to leave one firm and go to another. But the corporation's existence still requires explanation – especially in moral terms.

As R H Coase pointed out in 1937, the existence of the firm is a response to transaction costs.[24] If every carpenter, painter and toolmaker freely contracted with other, separate agents, this might preserve individual liberty but it would involve tremendous costs, the costs of making the necessary transactions. However, if all relevant employees are gathered together in one organisation this intensifies the division of labour and eliminates the need for cumbersome and costly individual contracting. Every person works for the organisation. When a person contracts into a given firm it is, of course, a free act, but the organisational structure of the company reduces typical market liberties. There are, however, great efficiency gains for the firm and society at large. According to the Coase model, a given firm need not be a permanent form of economic organisation; whether it or the pure market exists will depend on transaction costs, and these could change over time.

What makes the firm an issue for business ethics is the fact of the corporate form. The limited liability corporation is said by critics to have certain privileges that it acquired from the state. Apparently these would not have emerged from the individualistic market, subject to private property law and the law of contract; they could only have come from statute. The privileges that business ethics have in mind are perpetual life, recognition of the corporate form for the purposes of law and, most importantly, limited liability for debt and for tort actions. The 'privilege' of limited liability, by which owners are only liable for what they have actually invested in the corporation and not for their private wealth, is the most contested feature of the corporation. It has always been said that the corporate form could not exist without these privileges. Corporate rights are different from individual rights and without the former, capitalism could not operate successfully. It would be reduced to a collection of owner-managed enterprises and partnerships; the giant corporations of modern capitalism would be absent. The business world therefore has to 'repay' society for its generosity.[25] This is the foundation for the supererogatory duties mentioned in chapter one.

The 'concession' theory of the corporation – the doctrine that all the features of the corporation are grants of privilege conceded by the state – is not confined to arcane texts on business ethics but has a resonance in public policy debates. In a speech in 1996, the secretary for labor in Clinton's first administration, Robert Reich, said: "The corporation is a ... creation of law. It does not exist in nature".[26] In return, he said, "it is only reasonable to ask corporations to be more accountable for the costs and benefits of economic change". What Reich and others were concerned about was the apparent insouciance of corporations to certain consequences of the rapid economic change in the United States in the 1980s and 1990s, notably 'downsizing' (reducing personnel), relocation of plant, middle-class unemployment and the dramatic changes in working practices brought about by the technological revolution.

RIVAL CONCEPTIONS OF THE CORPORATION

The classic free-market view of the corporation is that it is an economic entity which emerges, *contra* Reich, through natural processes. The corporation is a legal entity only in the sense that conventional common law processes, namely contract, have generated an agency that has no more rights than do private persons under that same legal regime, and, by the same reasoning, the corporation has precisely the same legal rights and duties as private persons. In modern liberal democracies corporations operate under company law. But it does not follow from this that companies need the statutory codes, any more than it follows that because we all now have to accept the state's money, that is the only way a common currency could exist. Private alternatives can be envisaged.

The market view of the corporation, therefore, is that of a voluntary organisation, constituted by individuals who agree to pool their assets and form a body that acts collectively for specific purposes under common law. The corporation takes on burdens shared by its individual members, and the owners of the enterprise so created are entitled to the residual profits. The joint stock company appoints managers who have a strict fiduciary duty to the owners of the enterprise. If it is big enough, the limited liability company can get a stock market listing and its shares are publicly traded, but this makes no difference to the relationship between employees and owners. The fact of size does not suddenly make the directors of a limited liability company responsible to 'society' rather than to the legal owners. The common law, then, does not create corporations; it merely gives legal recognition to those that are created by individual contracting. From this perspective, the so-called privileges of the corporation are not privileges at all, but are economic advantages negotiated *via* common law between parties for their common benefit. For example, no one has to trade with an organisation that declares by contract that its liability will be limited to its members' actual investment. Limited liability for torts is not actually required for corporations to function – especially big organisations which could stand losses. Smaller ones could always get insurance, perhaps as a condition of recognition. Perpetual life of a limited liability company is something of a myth. Although the personnel of a corporation change over time and it may sometimes be difficult to identify members in the case of responsibility for corporate wrongs, none of this is sufficient to dilute the company's individualistic foundation. As Robert Hessen has said, "at every stage of its growth the corporation is a voluntary association based exclusively on contract".[27]

There is confusion over the history of the corporation. In the early stages of its development in England it was a creation of the Crown and was not specifically commercial. It was endowed with special privileges, and therefore did have statutory duties. Later, in both Britain and the United States especially, the corporation emerged through common law processes.[28] In Britain the commercial corporate form was forbidden (after the South Sea Bubble scandal) and later it was only possible by statute. However, this situation was regrettable because it gave the impression that this was the only way a corporation could exist, and provided the excuse, therefore, for excessive state regulation.

In the United States, the corporate commercial form was given legal recognition in the nineteenth century and developed rapidly. In this model of the corporation, the responsibility of the board of directors and the management was to the shareholders – this is the meaning of the expression *fiduciary duty*. This is still the case in the commercial law of the English-speaking world. But there is a movement, with some New Zealand supporters, which holds that this fiduciary duty should be extended to 'society' – that business agents and entities other than the owners should have some claim at law if the corporation fails to fulfil a socially desirable role. Adrienne von Tunzelmann suggests that "directors may in fact be in breach of their fiduciary responsibilities if they are not taking care of key relationships, including community interests".[29] She is echoing a report by the Royal Society for Arts called *Tomorrow's Company*,[30] which specifically departs from the traditional view of business responsibilities. Such sentiments are regularly presented in anodyne language. The claim is that the recognition of corporate responsibilities will actually increase the long-term profitability of companies. This may be true, but whether or not it does so is a matter for the market and for the individual judgment of shareholders and their managers; such action ought not to come from the prescriptions of business ethics.

The separation between ownership and control, which is a feature of the modern business corporation, makes no theoretical difference to corporate responsibilities. Managers are not independent – they are not in control of fiefdoms beyond any kind of supervision. They do, however, have a great deal of discretion in the day-to-day organisation of their companies, but such independence is always limited by the legal'duty of managing the assets in the interests of the owners. The principals (the owners) and the agents (the managers) are in a complex relationship that is ultimately controlled by the market, and the market for corporate control, that is, the takeover mechanism, is the ultimate sanction for those managers who do not fulfil their legal, economic and moral duties to owners.

It is also sometimes argued that the owners of corporations do not have final discretion over the control of the assets. Griffiths and Lucas[31] claim that ownership is not decisive, as the formal owners simply own the shares – the company itself is not owned by them and is limited by a network of legal and moral duties. Owners cannot authorise managers to pollute the atmosphere in the pursuit of profit or turn the company headquarters into a brothel. Such legal restrictions apply to any business agent – they do not imply any *special* restrictions on the right of the owners to the residual profits of the enterprise. The distinction alluded to is a distinction without a difference. The real owners of a company become known in the event of a takeover offer – they can sell their shares to the highest bidder. The restrictions that have recently been placed on takeovers are arbitrary interventions (often introduced at the behest of managements) which are antithetical to the interests of owners and the purposes of business.

Business ethics activists rarely comment on what is morally significant in the principal-agent relationship: the fact that the relationship itself gives managers opportunities to neglect their fundamental duties. Managers may for example, engage in rent-seeking activities. In any successful commercial system 'economic rent' is created. This is the income earned by factors of production over and above that required to bring them forth. This 'extra value' is a feature of all successful enterprise, and the temptation is for managers to appropriate it for themselves in the form of perks and other advantages, in addition to salary. Owners may wish to encourage internal entrepreneurship through share options and other incentives, but managers may also search for this economic rent through *opportunism* rather than productive activity. This entrepreneurship is likely to be a feature of enterprises that have a low degree of trust between the owners and managers. Extra costs will therefore be imposed on owners who then have to respond by using expensive monitoring techniques. Managers tend to be well-disposed to companies pursuing supererogatory duties – acting for the community may be easier, as well as morally more pleasing, than working for the shareholder. Opportunism, the seeking of (not necessarily illegal) advantages from human interaction, is a feature of all social relationships, including marriage and divorce.[32] Contrary to the blandishments of business ethics, human nature never changes.

There is a difference between private limited companies and publicly listed companies (alluded to earlier) which has great significance for business ethics. A public limited corporation is responsible to shareholders, often widely dispersed, who invest precisely to secure the highest possible monetary return. The shareholders do not make the investment to secure some moral goal, although ethical investment trusts are perfectly appropriate vehicles for persons who wish to make investments consistent with their moral beliefs. In capitalist economies, like Britain and New Zealand, the majority of equity is held by institutional investors, insurance companies and pension funds, which makes the economic and moral obligations of company managements to owners even more pressing. These institutional investors have, in turn, strict fiduciary obligations to the millions of people who have entrusted their funds with them. It would be a gross dereliction of duty on the part of institutional investors if they were to allow investment decisions to be governed by what are, in effect, subjective decisions about the morality of the activity in which they are investing.

Privately owned companies can make their economic decisions depend on moral factors if they wish. Such an approach is promoted by the vocal and active proponent of an alternative view of corporate social responsibility in New Zealand, Dick Hubbard, who heads a privately owned company. Body Shop plc in the United Kingdom, a corporation with a very high ethical profile, has a policy of not using animal-tested products in its cosmetics business and is very concerned about the environment and the working conditions of its employees in plants in the Third World. For a long period the Body Shop showed a lack of concern about shareholder value. Eventually this led to a steep fall in its share price, as well as doubts about the reliability of some of its moral claims. The response of its founder and major shareholder, Anita Roddick, was technically correct: she considered taking the company private so as to be free from the pressure to maximise shareholder value.[33] However, the pressures brought about by bank debt promised to be just as onerous and the company was forced to continue as a stock market-financed business and even to promise to take more account of shareholder value in the future.

This example shows that there is little room for a *business* morality – as opposed to the exercise of moral judgments by individuals, including the shareholders of a business – that exceeds normal obligations to deal fairly, to honour contracts and to respect property rights in an efficient economy. If it is assumed that competition is a value itself for consumers and workers, the opportunities for extra-ethical business would typically lie in monopoly or in some other market imperfection. Company executives might well hope to ward off corrective measures by government by stressing their corporate virtue – a curious moral inversion.

The line of reasoning pursued here has a close connection with Milton Friedman's famous advice to company executives – that they should maximise profits subject only to the constraints of the "basic rules of society, both embodied in law and those embodied in ethical custom".[34] To go further, he says, is to arrogate for themselves a political role and, in effect, to be tax collectors. Elaine Sternberg goes a little further, arguing that if company executives pursue the recommended social goals they are guilty of embezzlement or theft.[35]

However, it is worth pointing out that there is a problem in Friedman's formulation, as the reference to 'ethical custom' is by no means uncontroversial. No doubt he wants to restrict ethical custom to the minimalist ethics outlined in chapter one, but unfortunately 'ethical custom' has become more expansive in recent years and there is growing opinion, which may have a degree of public support, that expects firms to do more than their legal requirements. Recent examples include public concern expressed over the treatment of the environment, and the 'rights' movements that have been pressing moral demands upon business. Ethical activists have become shareholder activists and attend annual meetings hoping to swing the boards of companies in an ethical direction. In May 1997, a shareholder resolution criticising the Royal Dutch/Shell company's record on human rights and the environment was presented to the annual general meeting.[36] It demanded rigorous compliance procedures and an external audit of the company. Shell has been in considerable trouble with environmentalists and human rights activists who have unfairly linked the company to the repressive measures of the dictatorial government in Nigeria. This particular resolution failed but, given the dispersed ownership of most publicly listed corporations, it might be possible for well organised activists to shift board policy away from maximising shareholder value. Also, given the recent public criticism of some business activities, it is quite possible that an appeal to conventional morality may not be as helpful to the business community as it was in the past.

It is possible that this ethical agitation may not actually represent general opinion; it may be another example of over-zealous moralists getting the plaudits for ethical action at little cost to themselves. However, the fact that western liberal capitalist society is pluralistic, and that that is one of its major virtues, suggests that business agents may need a more secure moral framework to work by than that provided by conventional ethics. Perhaps a more assertive demonstration is required of liberal individualism, and its underlying rationale, either in utility terms or in property rights logic.

Business leaders themselves are not averse to the fashionable re-orientation of ethics. In a survey undertaken in New Zealand by von Tunzelmann it was found that a majority of business leaders favoured an obligation of corporate responsibility which "lies beyond legal requirements"[37] and the application to community projects of "resources of the company which could alternatively [be] applied to other activities".[38] Naturally, such sentiments are wrapped up in qualifications, the most important being the claim that overall company performance would be advanced by exercises in social responsibility and that such activities might well pre-empt harmful governmental regulation (both of which considerations suggest that the activity is commercial or prudential, rather than moral in the proper supererogatory sense). However, it is noticeable that investment analysts in the von Tunzelmann survey were by no means as favourable to extended social responsibility as were the general business leaders, and how many of the latter would be so favourable if it were *their* money at risk? One suspects that surveys such as this are equivalent to opinion studies of voters which demonstrate that they would prefer a larger amount of tax to be collected for better public services. This is perhaps just another case of moral vanity – the same voters regularly punish in elections parties which do precisely that. When faced with a genuine choice, voters and investors are normally motivated by self-interest.

Behind this conception of business social responsibility that currently dominates the business ethics debate is a new notion of ownership. Owners of socially responsible businesses are not free to use their assets, within the constraints of conventional law, in the way that a private citizen can use their house, car or private savings. Rather, they must allow their resources to be used for a not uncontroversial conception of the public good. Owners of commercial enterprises are expected to become trustees of assets rather than genuine proprietors. This is quite clear from the currently fashionable propagation of the concept of the stakeholder, a topic that requires separate consideration.

THE STAKEHOLDER SOCIETY

The major rival to the shareholder responsibility theory of the modern corporation is the stakeholder theory. According to stakeholder theory the company consists of a network of participants who should have some say in the company's organisation and decision-making processes, irrespective of any formal property rights they may, or most likely may not, have in it. Since the participants are essential to the company's operation they must, according to the stakeholder view, be consulted about issues such as plant location, a takeover, redundancy, renumeration and so on. These groups comprise workers, suppliers, members of the community in which the company is situated and any other group that may have some connection to the company. Therefore, the list of potential stakeholders is almost unlimited. The term is applied to many fields, including welfare,[39] where every member of the community is considered to be a stakeholder and therefore entitled to some reward from the state irrespective of contribution. The development of the stakeholder society emerged out of a radical, quasi-collectivist theory of the firm. It also has a close affinity with communitarianism, a doctrine which is specifically anti-individualistic and which somehow sees all assets as vested in society rather than in traditional ownership structures.

Stakeholding is obviously a not very subtle play on the word 'shareholding' and its users try to capture some of the grandeur (that used to be?) attached to formal ownership rights. Its descriptive and normative usefulness is also readily explicable. All careful employers treat their workers in some sense or other as stakeholders – it would be a foolish resource owner who, for example, treated labour as eminently dispensable at the first sign of economic downturn. The firm may want to hire labour for the future and will want to avoid the reputation of being a heartless employer. This consideration applies especially to 'firm-specific' labour, labour that really has no alternative to the one in which it is presently employed. Likewise the firm will not want to dispense with a reliable supplier merely because some rival can (possibly temporarily) provide wanted goods and services at a slightly lower price. The firm must think of the long term, when predictability is all-important. Furthermore, relationships with the local community are commercially important and the sensible owner will not wish to alienate local citizens on whose custom the profitability of the firm may depend. This is especially important in environmental matters. But these are the actions of the prudent business person, not the prescriptions of some heady moral philosophy.

The stakeholder theory, however, now means a lot more. In effect, it subverts the ownership structure of the firm and disrupts the resource allocation mechanism of the market. It is socialism by another name. What is most noticeable is the crude egalitarianism that inspires it. It would seem that all stakeholders have a *prima facie* entitlement to a managerial role: plant relocation could not take place without the consent of strategic stakeholders (in practice, they would be those adversely affected by such decisions); employment and redundancy matters could not go ahead without the approval of certain well placed groups (normally trade unions); and a myriad of other decisions which should be determined by the market and the decisions of owners would also be at the mercy of people who had no *financial* stake in the enterprise. The behaviour of corporations would be subject to political pressures equivalent to those that operate at the parliamentary level. Indeed, it is no coincidence that stakeholder theorists regularly call those groups that press on the firm, *constituencies*.

To be socially productive the relationships between the participants in an enterprise must in an important sense be unequal, and that inequality will then be a function of how much property those participants have invested in the enterprise. Those people who put up the capital bear the risk and so are entitled to any residual profits. They, and the wider community, will be adversely affected if non-economic factors are allowed to influence decisions. Shareholders in a market economy have no protection for their resources except the efficient functioning of the firms in which they invest. Employees and other stakeholders have a number of defences against the vicissitudes of fortune, such as legal contracts and alternative contracting opportunities. Shareholders have only their capital that may well be rendered worthless if stakeholder theory were taken seriously.

Again, stakeholder theory is internally incoherent. It cannot provide an organising device for the coordination and settling of disputes between potentially rival stakeholders (each with an equal right to be heard and to have their views considered). Which stakeholder group is relevant in a plant relocation decision? Present employees who will have their lives disrupted by the move, or potential stakeholders and residents in the new location whose employment prospects and life chances will be badly damaged if it does not take place? Who should be made redundant in an unavoidable downturn? Those whose marginal productivity is the lowest, or those who have an influential voice in management? It is certain that rival coalitions of stakeholders will form groups whose actions will not be a product of economic rationality but a function of their respective quasi-political strengths. Stakeholder groups have had a particularly deleterious effect on takeovers. The anti-takeover measures adopted by various American states were ostensibly driven by communitarian principles, but in reality they were instigated by managements fearful of losing their jobs in the event of major corporate restructuring. In Germany, the economically feasible Krupp takeover of Thyssen was resisted by a coalition of management, unions and community groups.[40] It became a tame merger.

To some, the price mechanism may be a crude measure of a product's value but it is the only measure we have that provides predictable and objective answers to the typical problems of the modern firm. No exquisite Rousseauistic 'general will' could emerge from the deliberations of stakeholders, only the incessant squabbling of selfish groups. Squabbling and factionalism are quite different from the benign effects of individual self-interested actions coordinated by the market and subject to common law rules.

In an influential article on stakeholder theory, Evan and Freeman, in their explicitly moral theory of the corporation, show some recognition of the stakeholder problem, although their solution is risible. They realise the importance of ownership while systematically downgrading its significance. They write: "The reason for paying returns to owners is not that they own the firm, but that their support is necessary for the survival of the firm, and that they have a legitimate claim on the firm".[41] However, their position is, apparently, on a par with any other stakeholder. It is an explicitly Kantian theory in which a rarefied notion of 'duty' takes precedence over the economic rationale of ownership. To the charge that little agreement is likely to come of negotiations between all the stakeholders, Evan and Freeman suggest that the firm should appoint a 'metaphysical director' who would impartially adjudicate between all the claimants. This is little more than rent-seeking by philosophers who would have every incentive to dispense with the price mechanism. Such a 'director' would prolong the intractability between rival stakeholder groups up to the point at which the corporation just avoids bankruptcy. Who would entrust their assets to a firm organised on such principles?

Even in a less malign form, stakeholder theory poses a serious threat to the rationality of the corporation. Suppliers of capital are in effect being used as a means to the ends of others, not those of well meaning but unsophisticated moral philosophers but the short-term goals of purely selfish private groups. The situation could become even worse if sections of society, which have no connection at all with the enterprise, were able to have influence and representation on boards of directors. These would be groups representing the 'community', the environment and any other 'cause' that attracts political attention. Such representatives would no doubt be called 'independent', but this is very different from the independence of directors from managers, or that of certified accountants charged with the audit of the organisation. These representatives would most likely have agendas dictated by various virtuous, and anti-profit, groups.

CORPORATIONS AND THE COMMUNITY

As outlined previously, in return for their alleged privileges corporations have been encouraged to forgo profitable opportunities and 'give something back' to the community. Social contract theory is often invoked.[42] A hypothetical contract between business and the community is envisaged in which profit-seeking business agents provide something for the people at large as a 'price' for the permission to produce and to trade. It is not enough for the market to provide jobs and goods, it must also contribute to the locality in the form of welfare and other projects. However, the analogy between contract law and business *and* society is misplaced. There has never been such a contract historically and it makes no theoretical sense for such a contract to exist. The community cannot be conceived as an agent with an ordered set of preferences that can be satisfied through an exchange with, in effect, private groups. Society consists of a myriad of subgroups each with its own agenda and, when it comes to business largesse, each has a different set of demands that cannot be coherently ordered. The problem is exactly the same as that confronting stakeholder theory: the impossibility of adjudicating between sectional demands.

Business ethics, however, makes supererogatory claims on business. The tendency now is not to treat these duties of corporate responsibility as some kind of 'add on', an addition to the normal profit-making activities of business – perhaps to buy favours from its critics or to forestall regulation and control – but as an integral part of the company's 'mission'. Business policies that aid the community, for example making grants to public and charitable bodies, aiding deprived groups or contributing to educational institutions, should be seen as being as necessary for the company as are the plans to launch a new product or to embark on an advertising campaign. Whether such activities actually contribute to the corporation's 'bottom line' is a matter for the market to decide. Given the discretion that managements have in determining business strategies that are most likely to advance shareholder value, it is impossible to say *a priori* that these activities will fail, but a healthy dose of scepticism is in order. However, since part of the rationale of the business responsibility thesis is that there is often a compelling case to pursue such projects, even if they do involve a reduction in profit, there is the possibility that a clash will arise between business rationality and business ethics. Spokespersons for this point of view also often mention the threat of the withdrawal of business 'privileges' for those who do not cooperate or the offer of tax breaks and other advantages for those who do (this is openly recommended by Robert Reich).[43] It is, however, a curious kind of morality that can only be persuasive by threats or bribes.

Shareholders, at the very least, should be involved in decisions that may reduce profits. It is hard to imagine that if corporations were to become involved in community activity of the sort prescribed there would always be a monetary benefit to the owners. The initiative for these activities always seems to be a matter for the managements to take – the people least likely to be harmed by them. The managements are also likely to benefit in terms of moral esteem and an easier life. The admission of these community activities as being equivalent to fiduciary duties or actions taken in the interests of shareholders, as interpreted in a broad financial sense, would amount to a revolution in business law. From a purely moral perspective, who is to be the subject of business benevolence? What principles of distributive justice should determine the allocation of the rewards?

In New Zealand some business moralists have been attracted to proposals of this type. They have clearly been influenced by American counterparts, and the organisation New Zealand Businesses for Social Responsibility is allegedly modelled on a similar American organisation.[44] No doubt the new-found freedom from some oppressive regulations enjoyed by New Zealand businesses in recent years, and the open encouragement given to entrepreneurship, have been influential in the moral introspection that now characterises business. However, the danger is that this moralism may well divert business from its primary obligation. That obligation is the observance of the duties to shareholders, the pursuit of profit, the satisfaction of consumer demands and the drive for efficiency that have contributed to the triumph of western capitalism as an unrivalled mechanism for raising living standards, especially those of the poor. Lessons here could easily be forgotten in the current desire to be virtuous beyond the requirements of traditional law and morality.

Business moralists should also be aware of the unintended consequences of supererogatory ethics. Henry Manne provides an instructive example of this from the early 1970s.[45] Coca-Cola operated a plant in Florida in which working conditions were particularly bad. (Note that most of Coca Cola's employees were from the Third World where working conditions were much worse.) Under moral pressure, the company implemented a kind of private enterprise welfare system. However, the costs of running this system reduced employment opportunities for newcomers. The moral action was noticed – it was after all highly visible – but the ensuing unemployment was not. This type of situation is a feature that recurs in business. Morality, for good or ill, is seen and can be attributed to named persons or groups – economic effects are not seen[46] and the causal agents responsible for these effects are not directly identifiable.

CORPORATE MORAL WRONGS

The critical concern with supererogatory morality should not distract us from the fact that business wrongs do take place and they are the proper concern of business ethics. There have been a number of well publicised scandals in Anglo-American capitalism in the last 30 years or so, although it should be pointed out that they are typically less venal than those that have occurred in the allegedly more moral, and less greed-driven, communitarian capitalist systems. Japan has been replete with examples of gross business immorality. It is partly a tribute to the open nature of Anglo-American capitalism that such cases of moral turpitude have been quickly exposed. In the more enclosed worlds of Asian business the scandals can be hidden for long periods of time. The Tokyo stock market is a good example, because within it the lack of concern for shareholder value, and the derisory influence that investors have on companies, have enabled corruption to be concealed. Some stock market scandals have involved reputable broking houses.[47] Anglo-American economies are much more open and transparent than their rivals, as is easily seen by a comparison of the disclosure rules for public companies on Wall Street with those in Frankfurt. There may be a connection between this feature and the traditions of a free press and general liberality, although a causal connection would be difficult to demonstrate.

BUSINESS CODES

Self-regulation by business is probably the most efficient and just method for the enforcement of moral standards. It is in the interests of commerce that business adheres to sensible conventions. This is undoubtedly the reason why business codes of practice have become a popular mechanism of moral persuasion. Individual employees are more often responsible for unethical conduct than corporations themselves. Corporations, after all, are not established as criminal conspiracies; the case of the Bank of Credit and Commerce International is a remarkable exception.[48] However, an organisation can be held responsible for an individual employee's actions if it does not take measures to prevent wrongdoing. In the famous case of British Airways and Virgin it is noticeable that British Airways did not have a business code of practice, although most companies listed on the London Stock Exchange do.[49] British Airways did not have any mechanisms in place to deter over-enthusiastic employees. In the much more spectacular Robert Maxwell case, people continued to trade with the company, and to lend Maxwell vast amounts of money, when his unethical practices had been exposed by a British government departmental enquiry and he had been condemned as unfit to head a public company.[50]

It is not surprising that individual malefactions should occur in the corporation. Internal entrepreneurship does take place within the firm and is rewarded accordingly. It is simply a matter of moral symmetry that individual wrongdoing should be punished, although there is a regrettable tendency, especially in American law, for corporations to be treated as moral agents, capable of committing criminal offences and subject to the *mens rea*.[51] This tendency is not only an illegitimate attempt to attribute personhood to artificial collective entities, but it also allows the individual wrongdoers to evade responsibility. If business codes could completely deter unethical behaviour they would be admirable and remarkable, but the institution of these codes is not necessarily the solvent for all the problems of business ethics. Both pro- and anti-business writers have been sceptical, and even critical, of them.

Industry-wide codes however, must be treated with a certain scepticism as they are quite likely to be anti-competitive and may constitute at least one example of the spontaneous development of commercial rules that is not conducive to efficient markets. There is an inevitable tendency in human nature to seek rents and block out, through various kinds of conspiracy, more efficient rivals. The historical examples of this, especially the cartelisation movement in German industry that began at the end of the last century, have normally been helped by government intervention, most often through protectionism. There is no greater threat to anti-competitive behaviour than free international trade. Business codes should not be used to create pressures for political intervention.

Fortunately the business codes established in Anglo-American corporations have, in general, not displayed the same tendencies as the German codes, but there is always the danger that too great an enthusiasm for them might tempt industry leaders to try to 'close' the market by this method. A more plausible rationale for business codes relates to the need for commerce to protect itself against excessive government regulation – avoiding over-regulation necessitates some self-restraint. Business often has an informational advantage over consumers and exploitation of this advantage may fuel the demands for anti-business intervention. However, if they conduct their affairs according to a business code, all could gain. It would not have to be an industry-wide code that excluded outsiders.

The Code of Best Practice recommended in the Cadbury Report is an example of an approach which a company could take.[52] A code of practice puts ethical responsibilities clearly in the hands of directors (and also shareholders, including institutional investors). It is not strictly compulsory, though companies have to make a statement of compliance with it if they are to be listed on the Stock Exchange. (They might still be listed if they make a submission recording the reasons for non-compliance.) In a later article, Sir Adrian Cadbury expressed his preference for voluntary rather than statutory codes because the statutory codes specify minimum standards that companies might meet almost as a matter of routine. It is often said that codes of practice attenuate each person's sense of ethical responsibility since formal compliance might well reduce the incentive for moral rectitude in cases that fall outside the scope of the code. Sir Adrian does not, however, suggest that commerce requires a special kind of ethics; he rightly says "[B]usiness morality is personal morality writ large".[53]

Business codes have attracted the interest of business writers in New Zealand. Andrew O'Brien talks about 'engendering' the right attitudes in business, by which he means the cultivation of appropriate moral standards through a process of self-education.[54] This process would be preferable to rigid enforcement procedures that would be costly and unduly coercive. For example, a potential malefactor would be entitled to due process and justice, and given the opportunity to repent and reform. Still, one wonders why there should be that much concern about formalising morality, especially in New Zealand which has such a good record for business probity. Responsible business leaders have managed to avoid overly formal steps, and the Stock Exchange has not made a statement of the principles of corporate governance mandatory. The implicit suggestion from business ethics writers is that there is something special about business morality that differentiates it from ordinary ethics.

One possible reason for this concern is the disturbance to conventional collectivist values brought about by New Zealand's recent experience of a resuscitated capitalism. Former socialists have used the moral weapon to condemn business activity that fails to live up to impossibly high standards. A new wave of ethical enthusiasm is, superficially, more intellectually respectable than repeating the old anti-capitalist mantras. A good example of this enthusiasm is the witch hunt, instigated by a careerist politician, provoked by the alleged 'wine box' scandal.[55]

One undesirable consequence of attempts to moralise the corporation by an excessive use of codes is the disincentive to internal entrepreneurship that these codes may produce. Risk-taking and innovation are essential to a firm if it is to make efficiency gains. If enterprising individuals are required to constantly check whether or not their actions are consistent with a possibly arbitrary set of moral standards, internal entrepreneurship will atrophy and the corporate enterprise will degenerate into routine activity, which is a sure recipe for economic stagnation (that was New Zealand's experience under semi-socialism). It would be both ironic and distressing if the same outcome were generated by the voluntary methods of business itself.

THE FUTURE OF THE CORPORATION

Developments in Anglo-American capitalism may render the arguments about corporate social responsibility a little *passé*. It was noted earlier that in Coase's analysis the firm spontaneously emerged because of the problem of transaction costs. It is simply infeasible for each individual to negotiate, by contract, all the manoeuvres that are required for modern production. The myriad of multilateral contracts that are required has made the rise of bilateral contracts, through which employees commit themselves exclusively to one organisation, unavoidable and large-scale mass production inevitable. In earlier phases of industrial development negotiations between employers and trade unions about pay and working conditions were an obvious concomitant of the development of the firm.

Modern conditions and developments in Anglo-American capitalism may make the hierarchical firm a less decisive feature of the system than it was in the early days of free-market society. The emergence of the knowledge-based economy has made it much more practicable for individuals to negotiate private contracts, work from home, take on part-time work and be a lot more flexible work-wise than in the past. As well as this, skills can be marketed rather than commanded and directed. The Employment Contracts Act 1991 in New Zealand can be seen as a step in this direction.[56] None of this makes the Coase theory inapplicable; it simply means that transaction costs have altered so that it becomes much more feasible to use the market rather than the firm. What then does the notion of corporate social responsibility become? In a world where the market, rather than the firm, predominates, morality becomes openly what it really always has been, an individual phenomenon in the context of socially acceptable rules and conventions. Such trends are still largely prospective – factories and collective productive systems may well continue to co-exist with virtual firms – but it is a phenomenon that has been overlooked by conventional business ethics. This is a discipline that is still dominated by outdated, semi-socialist moral concepts.

Anglo-American capitalism is not one monolithic type – it is not a uniform system of business enterprise to which all commercial activities conform. Although the shareholder value model (in which managers and other employees are solely responsible to the owners and charged with the duty of maximising returns) forms a convenient contrast with alternative capitalisms, such as the German social market system and Asian communitarianism, there are variations within Anglo-American capitalism. For example, in addition to privately owned companies there are partnerships, producer cooperatives, and financial and other mutual companies, and although they all, to some extent, can be described as profit-maximising operations, the varying ways in which they function can have ethical significance. Some charitable activity can obviously be pursued by private companies without a breach of conventional fiduciary duties and it is already a feature of the established professions such as law and medicine.

Throughout the history of Anglo-American capitalism, great entrepreneurs, such as Cadbury, Rowntree and Nuffield in the United Kingdom and Carnegie, Rockefeller and many others in the United States, have given away vast amounts of money. None of these people was motivated by simple greed. The distinctive feature of Anglo-American capitalism is the great variety of institutional forms and behavioural patterns it has produced. This is a tribute to its openness and capacity to innovate. In other capitalist systems a certain uniformity is maintained, either by legislation or by social pressures, which usually has a particularist moral and, indeed, political goal. The much-maligned corporation of Anglo-American capitalism is simply one, albeit tremendously important, manifestation of the liberal, market system.

3
ETHICS AND THE
STOCK MARKET

Business ethics in Anglo-American economies has been greatly concerned with conduct in the stock market. The greatest scandals have occurred in the stock market, and in that arena the common concepts of social and political theory, namely justice, freedom and the common good, are used, sometimes as effective moral critical weapons but often as purely propagandist, anti-capitalist slogans. To the moralist there is something intuitively objectionable about mere 'paper shuffling' rather than the direct production of wanted goods and services. The activity of paper shuffling itself also seems to allow great opportunities for unscrupulous behaviour on the part of the participants in asset markets. It requires some sophistication to play the asset market game, a skill which ordinary members of the public are unlikely to have. Once again the problem of unscrupulous behaviour hinges on the question of knowledge, since great fortunes have been made because of asymmetric information. The market professional is almost certain to know more than the amateur, just as the company employee is bound to know more than outside shareholders, and it is a serious question whether these informational advantages amount to immoral exploitation of other people's ignorance or are a result of genuine skill and painstaking research.

There is a significant moral dispute over the extent of the claims of efficiency in business ethics. If the stock market allocates capital efficiently, so that everyone is made better off by its relentless operation, the utilitarian criterion of business ethics will clearly have been satisfied. The untrammelled capital market ensures that social and economic investments are optimal – they are a response to people's subjective wants for goods and services. However theoretically efficient the operations of the stock market might be, its practical working does raise questions of justice. These questions occur in two significantly different conceptual senses: in the procedural and the distributive notions of justice.

In the procedural sense, an economic process is just if it accords equal rights to all players, no one has an unfair advantage over another through race, sex or religion, no property rights are violated and no contractual obligations are breached. In principle, inequalities of talent and even initial resource endowment, if legitimately acquired, are not unfair.

However, the way that people behave, even within these rules, may be thought to give rise to charges of unfairness. It is here that the vexed question of insider dealing arises. It is maintained that someone in possession of scarce, price-sensitive information, which ought to be disclosed, has an unjustifiable advantage no matter how much the use of that information might contribute to efficiency. This possession becomes particularly important in the case of takeovers, where information about the intentions of bidders is at a premium and the fiduciary duties of employees, especially financial intermediaries, are compelling. Vast amounts of money can be made and costs to bidders raised to unnecessary levels because of an unauthorised tip (although to be really successful, insider dealings have to be restrained and discreet).

The request for justice in this situation is sometimes put in the form of the demand for a 'level playing field' – a thoroughly ambiguous concept. Does the profitable use of information by employees of public companies amount to a breach of moral and contractual obligations, the exploitation of the principal by the agent? This conception of justice raises questions of the legitimacy of property ownership and of the meaning and implication of fiduciary duty. However, in theory, the actual distribution of wealth that emerges from stock market transactions is not morally relevant as long as the procedural rules are complied with. But efficiency questions do arise when the compliance costs of regulatory justice have an adverse effect on resource allocation, which depends primarily on the gathering of information.[57] One suspects that the moralistic critics of insider dealing are motivated as much by the inequalities of wealth that the stock market generates as they are by procedural niceties.

Distributive justice, the rival concept to procedural justice, is specifically concerned with the outcomes of the capital market. Are the earnings of the major players consistent with an intuitive notion of fair reward? The vast salaries of some seem a world away from income according to desert (and a galaxy apart from income according to need). Some say that the particular skills deployed in the stock market have no genuine social worth but are only valued by an economic process that rewards a kind of self-defining notion of success. Surely, they say, an economy's efficiency does not depend on one person happening to be first, possibly by a split second, to a profitable opportunity, especially as the successful person often does not display what is conventionally understood as moral merit.

Unfortunately, although these concepts of procedural and distributive justice are analytically quite distinct, business ethics writers and law enforcement agencies often confuse them so that the fact of high earnings alerts over-zealous prosecutors to some possible procedural infringement. The remarkable earnings of Michael Milken, reported to be US$550 million in 1987, no doubt motivated prosecutors and led to his eventual conviction and heavy penalty for what were, in fact, quite trivial offences (they did not include insider dealing).[58]

There is another crucially important moral concept that is relevant to the ethics of the stock market: the rule of law. This fundamental feature of Anglo-American economies requires that laws be perfectly general, favour no one person or group of persons, be known in advance and be non-retrospective. It is clear that the excessive enthusiasm of prosecutors and their judicial creativity, especially in relation to insider dealing and takeovers, has compromised this concept. Such is the complexity and unpredictability of much of the securities criminal law and regulation that the players cannot know with certainty what is permissible and what is illegal in their industry. This is less true of New Zealand (see the last section in this chapter), whose securities law is limited in scope and is mainly civil rather than criminal, in comparison with the United States and Britain. Indeed, what were thought to be civil offences in the United States turned out to be criminal.

The reason why the morality of the stock market arouses such controversy in Anglo-American economies is that it is a crucially important institution for the raising of capital. The role of companies is to increase shareholder value for the owners, and managements have to constantly watch the stock market to make sure that the value of the corporation's shares does not fall so low that it becomes a takeover target. It is for this reason that concern is expressed over the morality of the stock market. It is felt that confidence in it would fall if outrageous examples of insider dealing were to occur; investors would be deterred through fear of having their funds at the mercy of unscrupulous market manipulators. In economies like Germany's, and most of continental Europe, where capital is primarily raised through bank loans, the pressure to maximise shareholder value is much less intense. In fact, share ownership is not widely spread in Europe compared with Britain and, especially, America. Insider dealing was never thought to be a problem in Europe and Germany had no law against it until the country was compelled to adopt a version of a European Directive very heavily regulating it in 1994.[59] Japan's economy is an interesting case because share ownership is quite widely spread, although the banks play an inordinately large role in corporate finance. However, under that country's communitarian capitalism the managements of corporations are not concerned with maximising shareholder value. The ordinary shareholder once depended on capital gains for returns, an expectation that has turned out to be sadly unfounded in the 1990s. The ordinary shareholder was in fact the victim of serious corruption and crime throughout the 1980s and 1990s when the meltdown in the Japanese stock market began.

Business moralists have made further criticisms of the stock market. They are reluctant to accept the measure of economic value that it represents because they feel it is based on people's subjective choices of goods and services. Companies that satisfy the desires of consumers will have good profits and high stock market values, but their goals may not accord well with the ideals of the moralists, or even with conventional moral standards. This subjectivism is, of course, technically true. The market satisfies the demand for sex and drugs as well as food, housing and clothes. Also, companies that despoil the environment for increased profits may do well on the stock market, as may those that manufacture arms for foreign dictators. This situation has led to the emergence of 'ethical' investment; trusts and funds that carefully assess a company's moral record before recommending the purchase of its shares.[60]

INSIDER DEALING

The most important feature of stock market trading is information, and the constant search for knowledge about the prospects of companies is the feature of activities by investment analysts, bankers, speculators and anyone else involved in the search for value in the market. Somebody who regularly beats the index has better information about company performance and a better 'feel' for the trends and sentiments of the market in general. Some of the relevant information is found in company reports and other published material which is available to anyone who makes the effort to find out, but other facts can be picked up in possibly quite innocent ways – for example from a taxi driver overhearing a conversation between company executives, or from friends or family members picking up gossip. As is often said, a scrap of undisclosed information is worth a year's solid research. Clearly, large sums of money can be made by people ('tippees') lucky enough to be in possession of vital facts, for example about a takeover bid, a new discovery or invention, in advance of their official revelation to the market. These are the well publicised instances of insider dealing, but it is likely that it goes on in less obvious ways.

The offence, if it is such, of insider dealing is simple enough to describe, but its ramifications are extremely complicated and involve difficult questions of economics, law and ethics. Insider dealing takes place when someone (an employee or any person closely connected with the firm or tipped off by an insider) buys and sells shares based on undisclosed knowledge (relevant information that has not been made available to the market) of a company's performance or future plans. Of course, there are many things which a company will not want revealed and its employees will be under a strict contractual obligation, even in a perfectly free market, to refrain from trading in its stock or tipping off outsiders. Under highly competitive conditions inside information is the most useful knowledge, but in circumstances well short of this all sorts of information that has market value is floating around. Questions of law and morality turn on who has the right to use this inside information.

Laws against insider dealing are designed to prevent insiders having an 'unfair' advantage over outside shareholders and are validated by some idea of equality of opportunity, or the goal of a level playing field. Some ideal of equality is met by the minimalist ethics of Anglo-American capitalism, which dictate that there are no arbitrary barriers to entry into the market and laws are applied impartially. Some enthusiasts for insider dealing say that outsiders can always join a firm if they really want inside knowledge, although this is not a particularly attractive solution to the problem of access to knowledge. Superficially, the ideal of a level playing field looks as if it is procedural, in that it merely specifies the conditions under which the game takes place. But the enterprise is now much more than this, because theorists are trying to establish such strict conditions of equality that many of the hard-won advantages earned by analysts through their research and contacts would be eliminated. Believers in a level playing field try to eliminate many of the vital conditions, especially in the gathering of information, that actually affect the outcome of the process.

These may be quasi-moral arguments but there are other sorts of considerations that relate to the issue of insider dealing that have more to do with property rights, efficiency and utility. Surely, it might be asked, should not the owners of a company, the outside shareholders, have the right to the information that might be acquired by insiders? It is, however, by no means obvious that such outsiders have an exclusive claim to inside information. Entrepreneurship takes place within the firm and it could atrophy if there were no opportunities for insiders to exploit their discoveries. The company is not only characterised by routinised production methods but also by alertness, innovation and flair. Should not this be rewarded with the right to trade shares? Historically, outside shareholders have not been in the vanguard of the campaign against insider dealing – most of the leaders have been politicians, administrators and moralists.

Moralism has fuelled the objections to the practice of insider dealing, and the ethical debate centres on the perennial controversy between utility and justice. Henry Manne, the most sophisticated opponent of statutory laws against insider dealing, openly condemns this moralism: "Morals, someone once said, are a private luxury. Carried into the area of serious debate about public policy, moral arguments are frequently either a sham or a refuge for the intellectually bankrupt".[61] Such a forthright statement is not an example of amoralism, or a plea for Mandevillian egoism, since Manne knows very well that the market requires some predictable rules, and he would argue that behind his claim for market freedom lies a version of utilitarianism. An unhampered stock market allocates capital efficiently, from which everybody gains. Manne's claim here for market freedom is based on utility and economic science. But a moral issue that concerns him is the threat to the rule of law that occurs from excessive regulation of the securities market.

What has undoubtedly powered the demand for tough regulation of the securities market in some countries is the wider spread of share ownership that has occurred in the aftermath of the privatisation of, until now, publicly owned assets. Without close supervision of the stock market and criminal sanctions (though in New Zealand insider dealing is not a crime), it was argued by regulators and others that private citizens would be defenceless in the anonymous world of high finance. More important, it is said that investors would be deterred from holding shares if insider dealing were to be permitted, although little evidence is ever produced for this proposition. Insider dealing seems to be a concern peculiar to Anglo-American economies precisely because most capital there is raised from the stock market.

INSIDER DEALING LAW IN THE UNITED STATES AND BRITAIN

Inspired by the moralism that accompanied the scandals involving the so-called 'robber barons'[62] and the stock market collapse in 1929, the laws against insider dealing originally developed in the United States through controversial interpretations of the Securities and Exchange Act 1934. The case that began the movement to regulate the market is a perfect illustration of the issues involved in insider dealing. In the mid-1960s a somewhat unsuccessful company, Texas Gulf Sulphur, made an important mineral discovery in Canada.[63] The people who had made the discovery delayed the announcement until they had bought stock in the company so that when it was finally publicised they made substantial profits. The original civil case against the Texas Gulf Sulphur Company was brought by the Securities and Exchange Commission (SEC) in the United States and it secured a conviction (in 1968) through an adventurous interpretation of Regulation 10b, made under the 1934 Act, which forbids the "employment of manipulative and deceptive practices".[64] It is not at all clear in this case that those involved in the activity were aware, or could have been aware, that what they were doing was illegal. The case provoked questions of property ownership, the nature of fiduciary duties and predictability in the law. To end the uncertainty about the practice, insider dealing was later made a criminal and civil offence by statute law in the United States. The SEC is responsible for bringing civil cases (which can involve heavy penalties) and the Department of Justice brings criminal prosecutions.

Although the new legislation, and the expansion of the SEC, generated a battery of controls, subsequent case law did something to establish principles governing the stock market in the United States. To be convicted, a trader had to be in a fiduciary relationship with the company, a director or someone else who held a position of trust, and had to gain from the transaction. Not surprisingly, the SEC has tried to widen the notion of fiduciary relationship. The situation becomes uncertain when the role of the 'tippee' (the person who first hears the information) is considered, because a long line of people (such as taxi drivers and lovers) can be interpreted to be in a fiduciary relationship merely by picking up scraps of information.

However, the US Supreme Court has clarified the issue of fiduciary relationships in a number of important cases. In *Chiarella v US*, Chiarella, a printer for a Wall Street publisher who uncovered information about a prospective takeover and traded on it, had his original conviction overturned on the ground that he owed no fiduciary duty to the seller of the shares he had bought.[65] Neither did he owe a general duty to the market (a favourite rationalisation of the moralists). It was not a fraud since there was no duty of disclosure. The mere fact of having the knowledge was insufficient. In the *Dirks* case, a financial adviser who knew that a company was about to be investigated for serious fraud and advised his clients accordingly, had his conviction overturned because he did not personally profit from the revelation.[66] However, there have been other cases in which the results are much less favourable to freedom of action and predictability of rules.[67] Fiduciary relationships remain a murky area with much uncertainty and some inefficient rules.

Notwithstanding these problems, in the well publicised scandals to do with takeovers the meaning of fiduciary duty is not in dispute. Ivan Boesky, the legendary arbitrageur, was convicted of offences involving insider dealing in the 1980s.[68] He had bought information about takeovers from an employee of various Wall Street investment banks, Dennis Levine. Levine was clearly in breach of his fiduciary duty not to reveal information – his doing so had adverse effects on the bidder. But all this could easily be dealt with by voluntary methods; indeed, investment banks have 'Chinese walls' that separate various activities that might involve their employees in conflicts of interest. The remedies for the misuse of information are available at the civil law level if threat of dismissal and shunning by market participants are not adequate deterrents.

In Britain, before the incorporation of the European Directive in the Criminal Justice Act 1993, the law was similar to that in America. Under the Company Securities (Insider Dealing) Act 1985, to be convicted a person had to be in a position of trust with a company. Although convictions were rare, one person was imprisoned[69] for selling his stock in advance of a big loss announcement and another, a financial intermediary, was heavily fined and given a suspended jail sentence for trading on knowledge of takeovers.[70]

Opponents of insider dealing regulation maintain that the problem, if there is one, could be solved by companies themselves. As Richard Epstein argues: "For a company to legitimise insider trading all it needs is a provision in its charter saying: 'if you want to deal in the shares of our company, please understand that every key employee and every director is entitled to trade on inside information to their heart's content. If you do not want to invest with us, you are free to buy shares in our competitor which does not allow that option'".[71] One would expect variety in the way companies deal with the insider dealing issue. Some might wish to restrict it to particular persons in the company as a way of rewarding them, but, if they did, outside shareholders under such circumstances could not complain of unfairness. Outside shareholders could sue under private law if the agreement were breached – if, say, every employee traded.

Unfortunately, the evidence from English private law is not encouraging for those wishing a non-statutory solution to the problem. In the only important case, where a shareholder of an unlisted company sued the directors who had profited from a takeover without announcing it to shareholders, the court ruled that they owed no such fiduciary duty.[72] However, it is not inconceivable that a fiduciary duty could be made explicit in the contracts of employment and constitutions of companies. The trouble now is that statutory law has replaced judge-made law in this area. In New Zealand, for example, actions for alleged harm caused by insider dealing have to be initiated by private persons, but this is done through statute law which embodies most of the restrictions and inhibitions that feature in countries which use public authorities for the prosecution of malefactors. The Securities Commission in New Zealand, although it promoted the insider dealing law, has no enforcement role.

The problem is that statute law in this area has meant that unending disputes, tainted by moral and political theory, have occurred and blanket solutions have been enforced. This has undoubtedly had a deleterious effect on information-gathering activity and on the system of predictable rules. It has led to rent-seeking and empire building in some countries by the public agencies responsible for enforcing the statutes.

THE CASE FOR INSIDER DEALING

The case for insider dealing derives entirely from the efficiency properties of free markets. Trading in shares is no different from trading in other goods and services, subject to the qualifications brought about by whatever voluntary restrictions the participants agree to enforce themselves. The control is achieved by the prophylactic effect of the market and basic law.[73] It is based on the assumption of the efficient-market hypothesis, that at any point in time the prices of securities exactly reflect the value of companies. Under these conditions, a 'random walk' effect operates, which means that it makes no difference what stock any trader chooses to buy, since all information is already incorporated in the stock's price. This is something of a theoretical ideal as there are always informational gaps to be exploited and the future value of companies is always a matter of uncertainty. The efficient-market hypothesis simply records the current value of a company – it cannot anticipate the future. The hypothesis states that at a given point in time the stock market accurately measures the values of companies but the consequent course of events remains unknown.

For the market to move towards the accurate pricing of securities, information must be allowed to circulate rapidly. The fewer restrictions there are, the quicker the information will flow and the lower the insider's profits will be. The relevant question for ethics is how that information circulates and what methods are used by traders. As we know, there is no problem in perfect equilibrium because there the assumption of perfect knowledge prevails. In situations short of this theoretical nirvana there will be, in ethics especially, disputes about the meanings of key terms, such as 'publicly disclosed' and 'relationships of trust'.

What the opponents of insider dealing legislation are objecting to is the utopian idea of a level playing field in securities markets and particularly the idea that statute law should reproduce this. If the level playing field refers to the ideal of equality of information among transactors, it is plainly absurd. Markets are normally only needed where there is inequality of information, otherwise there is little reason why anyone would exchange information (barring the exchanges that people with different preferences and attitudes to risk would make with perfect information). If there are no incentives for people who think they know more than the market to buy and sell, then the exchange system cannot play its coordinating role. Compulsory law here simply inhibits the search for knowledge and denies the successful a just reward for their efforts. In modern conditions it exposes them to the danger of unjust prosecutions.

Opponents of state regulation maintain that the criminalisation of insider dealing depends on the idea that the shareholders own all the property rights in the firm. However, entrepreneurship takes place within the firm and it cannot be assumed that the extra value created belongs exclusively to the formal owners, in the way that the office headquarters and the office furniture do. In an unhindered market the contracts between owners and employees would determine ownership, but statutory regulation of insider dealing reassigns property rights. Even apart from this consideration, there is the utilitarian argument that permitting insiders to deal in shares on the basis of undisclosed information creates a valuable incentive for internal entrepreneurship, from which the outside shareholders eventually gain. This quality is usually thought of as a feature of the great innovators of business history, but alertness to new opportunities and innovative activity is also common to employees, indeed it is a general feature of human action. If employees are limited to normal salary, bonuses and share options it may not sufficiently compensate them for their efforts and therefore be inadequate to motivate them. Why should the passive shareholder get all the value? Arguably firms and their employees should have the right to contract around these issues or opt out of specific insider trading law.

The literature on insider dealing has considered at length the notion of 'harm'. This practice is often labelled a 'victimless' crime. It is, of course, true that victims of insider trading may be hard to identify. After all, someone who lost out because, for example, a company insider dumped his or her shares ahead of a loss announcement might have sold anyway, and it is equally true that shareholders do not seem to mind price movements that can often only be explained by insider dealing. However, even determined opponents of statutory regulation concede that some harm does occur. Henry Manne says, "To the extent that insider trading does in certain circumstances injure particular individuals unidentifiable in advance, financial advantages flowing to all shareholders more than compensate for this loss".[74] This utilitarian argument would not satisfy the pure Kantian (or even adherents of the Pareto principle), but while some outcomes of market processes in general do involve harm to a few it would not be thought of as a sufficient reason for suspending the system. The more flagrant cases of insider dealing, which are likely to result in injury when an insider fails to disclose bad news, could be covered in contracts or the terms of a company's constitution.

A possible problem is that permission to trade on undisclosed information may encourage a person not to work for the company but to 'play' the market. The insider might be tempted to circulate false information and then 'short' the stock. Although it can be assumed that the market would soon sort out such unethical behaviour, there would be victims of the insider's activity before the market had time to perform its therapeutic role. There is no reason to suppose, however, that such anomalies and injustices could not be catered for in private law. Even if critics of the practice were dissatisfied with this – after all, it may simply be not worthwhile (and quite costly) for any single aggrieved person to go to law – any statutory regulation should be limited to reproducing the kind of result that would have occurred through private action. So far this has not been the case and state-decreed law has been much more ambitious.

There is also the suggestion that insider dealing might be technically inefficient. Market makers (brokerage firms that act as intermediaries between buyers and sellers and set prices), fearing insiders in the market, may price securities so as to protect themselves. They will widen the 'spreads' between the offer and the bid prices. This, of course, leads to inaccuracies in company valuation and a loss of confidence in the market. Still, there will inevitably be asymmetric information in the market, and there is little that regulation can do about this. It is noticeable that market makers often favour regulation of insider dealing because they are its potential 'victims'. However, market makers may not always be motivated by considerations of morality but merely want to preserve their rents. The alleged technical inefficiency may be becoming less of a problem anyway as stock markets, with the help of modern technology, are eliminating market makers because traders are increasingly able to deal directly with each other.

There is another difficulty that the most determined public regulator will find impossible to solve. What about insider dealing that takes place through the decision *not* to trade, as opposed to the deliberate act of buying and selling? Somebody might come into work on Monday with the intention to sell stock in the company because of a pressing financial commitment. They hear, quite legitimately, that the firm has secured a lucrative contract and defer the sale until the share price rises when the news is announced. They have secured a profit from undisclosed inside knowledge just as if they had bought stock. The morality is the same as for an original decision to buy or sell. Apparently, such phenomena are a substantial part of insider dealing. But how could they be regulated? It might be said that there is no reason to abandon the pursuit of obvious wrongdoers just because one can point to obvious examples of undetectable 'crime'. However, this begs the question as to whether insider dealing is properly a crime and it neglects the alternative, private-law solutions to the problem as discussed previously. Public regulation is as much about the fulfilment of social ideals, such as an extended notion of equality, as it is about righting wrongs.

CURRENT DEVELOPMENTS IN INSIDER DEALING LAW AND ETHICS

Recent trends in Anglo-American economies have not advanced the principles of insider dealing outlined above. The movement has been away from attributing legal and moral responsibility to those malefactors who have a relationship of trust with interested parties and allowing disputes to be settled within the framework of rules of private law. If anything, the trend has been in the reverse direction, with legislators trying to establish level playing fields and to blur the distinction between acquiring information by misuse of positions of trust within a company and genuine research (or even luck). Instead, legislation seems to be intent on making the possession of information, which others do not have, itself a reason for legal action and moral censure. The emphasis is not on a breach of fiduciary duty being a cause for legal redress but on the inequality of knowledge and how that inequality was achieved. New Zealand joined the international campaign against insider dealing in 1988 with the passage of its first legislation in the area (the Securities Amendment Act 1988), after previously leaving its stock market more or less unregulated in this regard. The restrictions introduced by that law stand in some contrast to the liberalisation that was proceeding elsewhere in the New Zealand economy. Perhaps the seemingly universal hostility to insider dealing, and the doubt about the general morality of the stock market, was driven by the experience of the crash of 1987 and by the moralism that has accompanied even non-socialist criticism of the market. Nevertheless, it is unrealistic to pretend that New Zealand was vulnerable at this time to dramatic share price falls because it did not have such stock market regulation.

A significant change in British law was introduced by the Criminal Justice Act 1993, which embodied the elements of a European Directive that had the apparently laudable aim of producing predictability and reliability in the securities market.[75] However, an examination of the legislation suggests that it might generate the opposite effect. Before the legislation was introduced, there had been some dissatisfaction with the state of British law. Since insider dealing was a criminal offence, the burden of proof was demanding and a conviction depended on the prosecution establishing its case 'beyond reasonable doubt', while in civil litigation all that is required is a 'balance of probabilities'. The success rate of the authorities was not good: between 1980 and 1994 (when the new Act came into force) the Stock Exchange referred about 180 cases to the prosecuting authorities but only 26 prosecutions were mounted and there were a mere 10 convictions.[76] It was apparent from cursory glances at price movements, however, that insider dealing went on. Yet instead of introducing a civil offence (as in the United States), or making it easier for actions to be taken under private law, the provisions of the criminal law were strengthened.

In brief, the new law introduced a number of innovations. It is no longer required that the information be confidential or, crucially, that a breach of trust must be proved for the prosecution to succeed. The accused must have had information as an insider (a shareholder, a director or someone closely connected with the firm, such as a financial intermediary), the action has to take place on a regulated market, the dealing must be in a specified and broadened range of securities and the information must be specific and not made public. The meanings of the terms related to insider dealing will depend on judicial interpretation. The controversial implication is that a person immediately becomes an insider if they happen to hear price-sensitive information, if it can be proved that it was non-public and if it is known to be from an inside source. The offence is not limited to dealing in the shares of a company in which the accused is connected but covers all share transactions in regulated markets. Since company employees will always know more about their own and related companies in general than outsiders, they will be under suspicion whenever any unexpected price movements occur.

Those likely to be most seriously affected by the new law in Britain are investment analysts who, in the process of providing advice to clients, search out information from a variety of sources. This information is almost certain to be non-public. The prospect of being suspected of insider dealing is likely to deter them from doing research and will prevent them from building close relationships with company officers through fear of being identified as an insider. There are some defences: for example, it is not illegal for companies to build up stakes in target companies in advance of a takeover announcement, and surprisingly – and contentiously – a person is permitted to deal if it can be shown that they would have done so without the inside information. Someone may have decided to purchase a house with the proceeds of a share sale and the deal will be legitimate even if the action is followed by a significant drop in the share price. It is not difficult to imagine some adventurous reasons being produced to explain particular transactions. A further, even vaguer, defence is one that permits the use of information that an individual has through being an insider but which does not prejudice the interests of others.

Because of these defences, the law is, in fact, not quite as draconian as it looks at first glance, but that is the problem. Convictions may be as hard to secure as in the past, which means that the real perpetrators of wrongs – those in breach of clear fiduciary duties – are not likely to be deterred, whereas risk-averse people will be. Already it is said that analysts will not talk to company officials unless they are in the presence of witnesses as these analysts are liable for criminal, not civil, action. Information is circulating less speedily and the City of London is performing its task of valuing companies less effectively.

LAW AND PRACTICE IN NEW ZEALAND

New Zealand is a latecomer to the public regulation of insider dealing. Prior to 1988 the matter was left to private law and aggrieved people could take action themselves and sue officials of a company who had breached fiduciary duties. There were some successful cases.[77] However, the stock market crash of 1987 and the unsubstantiated complaint that small shareholders were at the mercy of rich, slick operators, fuelled the demand for tougher regulation. The campaign coincided with the international furore about morality in the stock exchanges. The result was the Securities Amendment Act 1988.[78]

It is noticeable that the background to the 1988 law did not include any sustained cost-benefit analysis of securities legislation. Commentators have cast serious doubt on the value of public regulation to the efficient operation of the market as an information-gathering device. The new law is almost entirely a response to public pressure based on little practical knowledge. Many informed observers are highly sceptical of the statute. Those who favour regulation doubt that the law stops insider dealing. Price changes up to the announcement of a takeover (the major sign of insider dealing) seem to go on as before, and opponents of the statute say that it is cumbersome, damaging to research into securities and costly. New Zealand, unlike Australia (and most of the English-speaking world), does not have a criminal law against insider dealing. It is entirely a civil matter and actions have to be undertaken by private persons. In New Zealand there is no civil prosecuting body equivalent to America's SEC. New Zealand has the Securities Commission, which is responsible for the administration of legislation affecting securities, but it does not bring cases to prosecution.

Despite these important differences, New Zealand's 1988 Act does embody some of the principles that have been found to be so unsatisfactory in other Anglo-American jurisdictions. The legislators of the statute seemed to have been influenced by the idea that all shareholders should have access to the same information. However, as has been shown in relation to other jurisdictions, access by all shareholders to the same information is an impossible ideal. Information will always be asymmetric and the differences between the knowledge agents have does not typically imply wrongdoing or breach of trust. An agent's level of knowledge will often reflect differences in skill and ingenuity in gathering information. Also, for good commercial reasons, there are types of information that companies will not want to make available to the market. However, as with tough securities laws in general, the rewards are great for those people who really do cheat and profit from information that should have been revealed to the market.

Under the Securities Amendment Act 1988, insiders are defined as the public issuer, directors and any officials of the company and professional advisers who possess price-sensitive, non-public information. They are liable at civil law if they buy and sell stock in advance of a company announcement. They may not encourage others to trade (the practice of tipping) and immediately become liable if they do so. This provision creates a difficulty for professional advisers who become insiders merely by doing their job. It seems that the law is not targeted at people who, say, tip on receipt of a bribe, but at anybody who happens to know something. Liability also arises when an insider uses information about another public issuer of which they are not an insider. People making enquiries under the 'due diligence' obligation could also find themselves insiders and liable to civil law. There is an exception in relation to takeovers where the buyer of the target will obviously be in possession of some inside information, but the exemption does not apply to the seller or its advisers. They become liable if they make information available to potential bidders. How can directors fulfil their duties to shareholders and how can professionals do their job competently if such a restrictive regime were to be rigorously enforced? Those found liable under the law have to pay three times the value of their gains or three times the value of the loss avoided through their insider dealing.

Fortunately, the Act has so far not been rigorously pursued, although it might have had some deterrent effect. At the time of writing there has been no successfully decided insider dealing case in New Zealand.

Perhaps because so much of the unlawful stock market activity as defined by the Act is part of everyday trading practices involving no dishonesty, professionals are reluctant to bring actions, especially in areas where the law is thought to impede conventional modes of behaviour.

What is distinctive about the New Zealand legislation is that it is enforced by private individuals who may have been harmed by insider dealing. The action, however, has to be funded by the issuer, even though it may have no financial interest in the proceedings. A former member of the company who was a shareholder at the time of the alleged infraction may also take an action, again to be funded by the issuer. As Roger Partridge has pointed out, this is really a tax on the issuer.[79] There is an obvious danger of 'moral hazard' here (moral hazard occurs, for example, in welfare policy when a provision designed to help the unfortunate simply encourages others to become unfortunate). Without a financial constraint, aggrieved former shareholders could be expected to multiply. The problem will be compounded if a recent recommendation of the Securities Commission were to be accepted. This would remove the court's discretion in the award of costs and grant costs (paid for by the public issuer) even to an unsuccessful litigant.

Surprisingly, in the light of the above, there have been very few contested cases of insider dealing in New Zealand. It seems likely that many of the parties to a potential action do not have an incentive to pursue it. Still, the threat of legal action is always there, and its existence can encourage unscrupulous people to force out-of-court settlements. No one wants to be a defendant in a case, even if they have a good chance of winning. Apart from the financial costs if they lose, there is the opprobrium and loss of reputation that accompanies a court case. Thus, despite starting off with the inestimable advantage of not making insider dealing a criminal offence, New Zealand's legislation has nevertheless produced possibly the most unsatisfactory formal legal framework for securities trading in all the Anglo-American economies.

It is a pity that New Zealand has not extended its admirable free-market reforming zeal to formal insider trading law. However, it could be argued that changes to the law are not really needed as market participants manage to go about their normal activities quite successfully. New Zealand's situation is not as dire as, say, the City of London's, where there is a genuine fear that tough law inhibits the search for information. Nevertheless, ideally, New Zealand's legislation would be largely repealed and the regulation of insider dealing would be left to private law. The courts could be directed to regard information as the property of the corporation that has legitimately obtained it, and to allow a defence of proper use or proper purpose in using or releasing information selectively. As demonstrated from a number of jurisdictions, all of the moral problems to do with the activity of insider dealing could be dealt with in this way and, equally important, the efficiency losses that come from heavy state regulation could be avoided.

4

TAKEOVERS

There is a close connection between insider dealing and the takeover method of industrial reorganisation. Takeovers have involved some of the biggest real and imagined scandals in Anglo-American economies, and a particular decade, the 1980s, has been singled out for the apparent rampant greed and anti-social behaviour of some market players. It was by no means the most takeover-driven decade in America's economic history,[80] but the spectacular nature of some of the deals and the lifestyles of the participants led to much excoriation and lampooning in Hollywood movies. The connection with insider dealing is obvious: share prices typically rise on news of a takeover and bankers and other advisers involved in the deal are under a strict fiduciary duty not to reveal information that could make the bid more costly. Some people succumb to the temptation.

In the takeover debate unflattering comparisons have been made between Anglo-American economies and those of continental Europe and Japan. In the latter, takeovers are not a common phenomenon, due, it is said, to the higher degree of trust that prevails between market players. Banks are the major shareholders and they seem to be engaged in long-term relationships with managements, who are less concerned about possibly ephemeral movements in share prices. Discipline is maintained over managements by more direct methods; there is said to be a greater sense of solidarity and the community's interests allegedly play as much a part in corporate strategy as do those of shareholders. In the English-speaking world, however, there is, apparently, distrust between market players. Shareholders think that managers may act in their own interests and become rent seekers anxious to build empires rather than return earnings to shareholders. Managers think that shareholders do not have the long-term interests of the company at heart and that they will sell out to a corporate raider at the first sign of a downturn. Contrary to much of business ethics, this distrust, when mitigated by the therapeutic effect of the market, is not harmful because the exchange system provides signals for all participants to adjust their behaviour to the exigencies of the moment. For example, the flight of German capital in search of higher returns outside Germany reflects the fact that inefficiency can result from tying up capital, often at the behest of unions and coalitions of stakeholders, in long-term projects. So-called 'short-termism' is not necessarily a commercial sin.

In the postwar years the takeover booms have taken two forms. Throughout the 1960s and 1970s some were driven not by the search for shareholder value but by managerial expansionism. Instead of returning extra cash to shareholders, managements embarked upon ambitious schemes of diversification.[81] There were very few synergies (the fruitful cooperation of different but complementary production units) in these takeovers. This led to the development of unwieldy conglomerates to which corporate raiders were alert. A predator like T Boone Pickens, for example, noticed that instead of embarking on new exploration projects, oil companies could extract extra value and more profit for shareholders from existing oil fields if they had better managers. It is strange that the business moralists concentrated almost entirely on the supposed malefactions and greed of the raiders and not at all on the breaches of efficiency criteria and ethical duties by managers (who ought to act in the best interests of the owners).

The controversy of takeovers relates also to the separation between ownership and control, which is a feature of the Anglo-American economies, because without the takeover mechanism managers would become the irresponsible 'autocrats' of critical anti-capitalist theory. The dispersed shareholder would be helpless against entrenched boards and managements that were immune to competitive forces. A different takeover controversy in New Zealand arises from the greater concentration of ownership of listed companies and the concern that small shareholders could be left at the mercy of large shareholders who may loot the company in the absence of protections against self-dealing.

The moral criticism of takeovers, although suffused with efficiency considerations, tends to be of two types. The first criticism, at the macro level, concentrates on the damage to the social fabric that is allegedly caused by the unrelenting and remorseless search for shareholder value. What has especially angered the moralists is the type of takeover that occurs when a raider (a 'shark') realises that money can be made from buying a profitable company and then breaking it up. Moralists do not realise that exactly the same logic drives the takeover process of an unsuccessful firm – a process to which, in some circumstances, the critics might not object greatly. Much of the moral censure here derives from communitarian social and political theory. The latter argument has, of course, been used in an entirely self-interested manner by managements in several states of America that were assiduous in pressurising local legislatures to pass restrictive laws in the aftermath of the takeover boom.

The second criticism, at the micro level, addresses the tactics often used – such as 'golden parachutes', 'poison pills' and 'greenmail' – in takeovers. A further complaint from the moralists is the level of debt (in relation to equity) that the predators sometimes generate. This complaint overlooks the fact that companies in economies that restricted takeovers often had much greater levels of debt. Also, the business moralists did not sufficiently appreciate the effects of tax advantages in most Anglo-American economies in favour of debt over equity, which is why takeovers were often debt financed.[82] No amount of moralising can overcome the (normally desirable) propensity for humans to respond to incentives.

THE RATIONALE OF TAKEOVERS

That takeovers are a method of disciplining managements (as well as a vehicle for industry restructuring and achieving other commercial benefits) and the potential for them creates a market in managerial talent. A prospective acquirer notices that the share price of a company is underperforming, thus signalling that the value of the assets is not being exploited sufficiently. They offer existing shareholders a premium above the current market price, acquire the equity and replace existing managers (who have every incentive to resist this). Once again, the process depends on the validity of the efficient-market hypothesis: the stock market values companies and transmits the information about firms through their share price. Critics often say that this undervalues research and development – investments which may take some time to be recognised by the market. However, this rationale ignores a mass of evidence that points to significant share price increases on the announcement of research and development plans by companies.[83] Even if this evidence were not decisive it is hard to imagine that governments, or coalitions of stakeholders, would have a better idea of future prospects than the market.

What is clear from all the empirical evidence, including that from Australia and New Zealand, is that takeovers add value, especially to the shareholders of the 'target' company.[84] The shareholders of the bidding company may not gain much, if anything, in the short term – this result is to be expected in a competitive market for corporate control. However, the measure of the bidding company's success would involve a longer period than just the time of the bid itself. It is also relevant to the assessment of the value of takeovers to pose the counterfactual: what would have happened to companies in the absence of a takeover?

The efficient-market hypothesis, however, does not tell us in which direction the market will move and where extra value will be created in the future. We need entrepreneurship for this. Following 'Austrian' economics,[85] and especially the ideas of Israel Kirzner,[86] it is possible to incorporate the theory of imperfect markets into the rationale of takeovers. The entrepreneur is not a resource owner – that is the role of the capitalist. However, the two features of market behaviour can be embodied in one person if that person has special skills relevant to market coordination: the facility of spotting gaps in the market, anticipating correctly consumer demand and organising the factors of production in new and innovative ways. It is the entrepreneur's ingenuity that gradually pushes the market towards equilibrium, a state of rest in which there is no possibility of further entrepreneurial gain. In reality this position is never likely to be reached and, if it is arrived at, any resting place is likely to be temporary and forever vulnerable to that uncertainty (and ceaseless change) which is a feature of economic life in advanced market economies. The entrepreneur may have no capital – that can always be borrowed – but does earn a 'profit' from insights into the market process. This is logically different from the income that is paid to a factor of production in a repetitive process and is a reward for alertness to new opportunities.

Not only does entrepreneurship have immense utilitarian value, since profit is the engine that drives the economy towards coordination, but it also has a moral justification deriving from rights. These rights ought not to be attenuated by contemporary ideas of social justice or reward according to desert – none of these has anything to do with the rationale of wealth creation. The discoveries of entrepreneurs are a type of property right to which the discoverers have full title. Kirzner uses the conventional moral principle of 'finders keepers' to validate pure entrepreneurial profit. Creators of value and innovators are normally regarded as morally justified in their claims precisely because without their enterprise the valued thing would not properly exist and, therefore, no one else could properly own it. (Oil under the ground is a physical, not an economic, asset until someone correctly anticipates that it will have value.) Some of this entrepreneurship will look like luck (a person may just happen to be first to discover something with seemingly little in the way of effort) but if rewards were fixed according to moral desert the economy would be opened up to endless (and subjective) disputes about who deserves what.

The real moral issues relate to the methods used by entrepreneurs in the discovery process. Kirzner himself discusses the possibility of disputes over ownership of discovered things. Who is entitled to the animal that is slain in a primitive society – the person who hits it with an arrow or the one who happens to come across the body?[87] Logically similar examples of dispute over ownership in advanced economies can easily be imagined. Further, ought not some things, for example water or other scarce resources with no clear ownership title, be considered to be communally owned (as indeed they are often are)?

Also, what is the difference between the exploitation of someone's ignorance and the creation of a genuine opportunity? What if your grandmother sells you for a few dollars an old picture which you happen to know is a Rembrandt? The case fits all the criteria of discovery described by Kirzner (she could have found out its true value herself). The deal is technically value-advancing. Even if we make a distinction between family ethics and business ethics, the logic of the example does make people wince a little for it points to a distinction between market ethics and what ordinary people may think about morality. There are certain rules that govern private relationships that would be inappropriate for anonymous markets. One suspects that the moralists are confusing the two realms.

These problems of disputes over ownership have a resonance when we look at takeovers, as this form of industrial reorganisation has many of the features of Kirznerian entrepreneurship. As noted above, the proper moral issues must relate to the methods and procedures that are used in value creation, rather than the outcomes of the process (which can include distributions of income and wealth that might not combine easily with some fashionable conceptions of justice). The corporate raider does discover something new, even if it is only the fact that a company's management is not realising the true value of its assets. Many of the takeovers of the 1980s consisted of precisely this. Buying up a company, selling off unwanted parts and putting new management in to run what remains is clearly an act of entrepreneurship that is a direct response to the uncertainty of the market. One can never know in advance whether the venture will succeed or not. In fact, some 1980s takeovers did not, which gave the activity an unjustified bad name in some circles.

The fact that many takeovers have been implemented with borrowed money is a further vindication of Kirzner's theory, because the successful entrepreneur has to persuade the lender of capital that the venture is worthwhile. The economic value lies in the ideas of entrepreneurs, not in the amount of capital they might possess. A lot of moralists worried that American corporations in the 1980s became weighed down with debt, but this fear has no justification in economic theory. There is no single 'right' relationship between equity and debt – a successful firm may be able to finance its operations very largely by debt.[88] There may in fact be an advantage in debt since, in the event of a bankruptcy, bondholders have a higher claim on assets than equity owners.

Many of the management buyouts that took place in the 1980s and have continued in the 1990s fulfilled one of the ideals of Adam Smith – the creation of the owner-managed enterprise. Entrepreneurial managers, wishing to be free of the constraints of shareholders and anxious to secure the full value of their contributions to the success of the enterprise, bought out the company on borrowed money, took it private and ran it exclusively themselves. They then brought it back to the market and realised large gains. These were not windfall gains (like an inheritance), but rather the fully justified rewards for their astuteness. Of course, problems with management buy-outs can arise, for example, their proponents may not reveal all they know so that they can buy the company at a price lower than its true value, but it is hard to imagine that investors would be deceived for very long, or very often, especially in a competitive market.

None of this is meant to imply that moral problems do not occur in takeovers when interpreted in the Kirznerian way. Doubts may very well arise over who made the discovery. A classic example in Britain was the so-called 'Guinness scandal' of the 1980s. Distillers, a liquor group, was known to be badly managed and to waste shareholders' money. It was a sitting target for a takeover but an expensive prospect. The first to attempt a takeover was James Gulliver of the Argyll Group. He did an immense amount of work on the financing of the deal and on the proposed reorganisation of the business. It was a costly deal and had to be financed by a share swap rather than by a cash purchase. The share price of the purchaser, therefore, had to be high.

However, Gulliver had a rival in Ernest Saunders of Guinness who originally came in as a 'white knight' to protect the company from Gulliver. But Saunders then went ahead with a serious attempt to take over the company and his bid eventually succeeded. He organised an illegal share price support scheme by persuading associates to buy up Guinness with indemnities and substantial success fees. There is some doubt as to whether organising a share price support scheme is always illegal – some people say that it is a regular practice in the City of London – but it is certainly a risky activity that could only have been achieved by the use of Guinness's resources. Saunders and his associates were eventually convicted and given heavy prison sentences.[89]

Even if Saunders and his associates had not been guilty of criminal offences there is still a moral doubt as to whether they were entitled to the gains from the takeover. Saunders did not discover the opportunity – he could, in fact, be said to have 'stolen' it from Gulliver. Martin Ricketts,[90] in a penetrating critique of Kirzner, makes an important distinction between discovering something and grasping it. He argues that there is a difference here which is not recognised by Kirzner, even though it is implicit in his example of the 'slain animal'. The person who makes the discovery may not necessarily be the one who actually profits from it. Who then owns the property right? Still, however indeterminate Kirzner's property right derived from discovery might be, it is difficult to see how a rule could be devised which satisfactorily distinguished between finding and grasping, unless the latter were the result of a straight crime. Undoubtedly many takeovers would be difficult to justify on anything other than the grasping principle.

Perhaps more tractable is the question of debt – an issue which emerged in the 1980s because of 'junk bond' financed takeovers. Although the junk bond was originally used to finance start-up companies that couldn't get funding in the restrictive debt market on Wall Street at the time, it was later used in some controversial takeovers in the 1980s, including the US$25 billion acquisition of RJR Nabisco by Kolburg, Kravis and Roberts.

The junk bond, developed by the innovative financier Michael Milken,[91] is not, in principle, controversial. It is simply corporate debt that cannot get an investment bank rating. The rating agencies in New York – Standard and Poor and Moody's Investor Services being the most prominent – are very conservative. Established blue chip companies tend to get high ratings, based on past performance, while up-and-coming companies, with bold schemes but no record of success, do not earn a rating at all. This reluctance to recognise them is derived in the main from the fact that they have had little time to build up a reputation for creditworthiness. Therefore to get credit these companies have to offer very high rates of interest.

Milken's genius was to discover that the default rate on non-investment grade bonds was remarkably low – in fact they were quite safe investments on average.[92] Another talent that Milken had was in discovering 'fallen angels', companies close to default that could be saved if appropriate management could be installed. However, what really frightened corporate America was the use of junk bonds to threaten the managements of established companies. Respectable banks on Wall Street that were unused to Milken's innovative methods were also frightened. Much of Milken's activity contributed to the corporate restructuring of 1980s America, and that in turn has contributed to the country's current economic success. The takeover boom did not lead to a concentration of ownership, a familiar complaint of anti-capitalist moralists. In fact, it led to the reverse: the break-up of large conglomerates and the emergence of more decentralised forms of ownership.

It is probably true that some of the methods used by Milken's imitators did not meet with the highest ethical standards – the pressure put on savings and loans institutions (building societies) to invest in junk bonds might be one example – and also some of the later adventurers did not have Milken's flair. The real perpetrators, however, of unethical behaviour were his persecutors. Almost every element of the rule of law was broken in his prosecution and eventual conviction: civil offences became criminal, witnesses (including Milken's family) were intimidated, and many other devices were deployed that would be instantly condemned if they were used in cases involving civil liberties. But Milken's treatment was not unusual in America's financial history.[93]

MORALITY IN THE TAKEOVER PROCESS

Some of the methods used in corporate restructuring have provoked considerable hostility, but it must be remembered that takeover battles are not quite like regular business activities. They are intensively competitive with not only vast financial interests at stake but also business and personal reputations at risk. Although many of the participants may know each other, the process still illustrates the relative anonymity of Anglo-American business. Relationships are basically contractual and lawyers and financial intermediaries play a significant role (they may have an interest in initiating takeovers). The threatened companies have every incentive to be as innovative in defence as the raiders are in attack. Indeed, the major ethical deficiencies are probably on the side of target boards and managements, though this is scarcely noticed by moralists.

A controversial tactic used by incumbent managements is the 'poison pill', which makes takeovers prohibitively expensive and raises serious questions about the control of companies. This practice is forbidden by the Takeover Code in Britain and in New Zealand, and its legality in America is a matter of dispute. With a poison pill the constitution of a target company is altered so that a group of shareholders has special rights which are triggered in the event of a takeover. The rights include special voting privileges and the right to buy and sell preferred stock at favourable prices. Since these are exercisable in the event of a takeover, they can make it extraordinarily difficult for bidders to succeed. Companies can, in effect, become bid-proof. Poison pills prevent open competition for a company, thus making it easier for a suitor favoured by the management to take over the company. It was the upholding of a pill by the Delaware courts in 1985 that, amongst other things, led to the decline of the takeover boom in the United States in the late 1980s.

The real ethical and economic problems arise when poison pills are put in place without the consent of the shareholders, as is often the case. The result has been a shift in the 'control rights' of companies towards management. Under the 'business decision rule', courts have granted significant discretionary power to managers in the day-to-day running of affairs, and they are assumed to act in the best interests of shareholders. However, if the ultimate right of owners to freely trade their stock is effectively attenuated, their control is seriously diminished and managers become *de facto* owners.[94]

Sometimes company owners may approve of a poison pill. They may wish to ward off a raider who wants merely to dismantle the company by selling off parts (a perverse form of asset stripping) when they think that more money over the long run can be obtained by keeping the company intact. But for good ethical reasons and sound business considerations, the future of the company should be a decision for the shareholders. Recent court decisions in the United States have lessened the effect of poison pills but they remain a serious weapon in the armoury of management.[95]

The granting of 'golden parachutes', favourable severance deals for top executives threatened with job losses in a successful takeover, has a rationale that may favour shareholders. Executives are in a strong strategic position to make the deal difficult so that bidders have good reasons for buying them off with what sometimes looks like very generous terms. Of course, managers may sometimes want to provoke a takeover to get golden parachutes, but once again it is up to vigilant shareholders to prevent such opportunistic behaviour.

'Greenmail', with its ugly connotations of blackmail, is perhaps the most controversial of all anti-takeover devices, but the sceptic is entitled to think that moralists are aiming at the wrong target, that is, greedy predators. The practice involves a potential bidder who has built up a small stake in a target company being bought off with a price for the shares that is not available to others. Often the company is loaded with debt raised to ward off the predator. It is a common plea of the moralists that all shareholders should be treated equally – the situation in New Zealand will be examined below – but it is by no means obvious that this should be the sole *desideratum* of securities law.

The real culprits in greenmail are managements anxious to preserve their own positions. The greenmailer is simply putting out a signal that a company is underperforming: a greenmail coup is often followed by a successful takeover. It is true that someone may go into the market with no intention of bidding for control but solely to extract greenmail (as sometimes happened in the 1980s). However, if this occurs, managements should simply refuse to pay and wait to see what happens. As in all the controversies over tactics in takeovers, the first duty of managers is to look after the interests of shareholders. The failure of managers to do this is the greatest immorality that arises in these situations. The predator is almost always depicted as the villain of the piece, but in reality it is often the underperforming managers. They are normally better at public relations and particularly adept at appealing to the 'community' in the propaganda war that often features in takeover battles.

TAKEOVERS AND THE COMMUNITY

The idea of 'community' suffuses current debate about social values in the west. It is not exactly a surrogate for failed socialism, but certainly the anti-individualistic prejudices of socialism are reproduced in what is claimed to be a new philosophy. Communitarians argue that the notion of the abstract individual is intellectually incoherent,[96] but also that public policy should be geared towards the preservation of intimate and more meaningful social structures that are threatened by the ravages of market individualism, a morally respectable motivation often dismissed as egoism. Communitarianism stresses the particular and local (in terms of rules and social institutions) while capitalism and the market are remorselessly universal – their very openness and indifference to cultural background are among their many virtues.

A quick glance at world capitalism suggests that the communitarian claim is very odd since the market system has prospered in a wide variety of cultures. Does anyone really suppose that the relentless progress of the market in Asia (despite its current travails) has needlessly eroded socially valuable communal structures there? The communitarian seeks to obtain the advantages of capitalism without a loss in the warmth of collective values. The takeover mechanism is particularly reprehensible since it is the most obviously individualistic feature of Anglo-American capitalism and because other successful (if not equally so) market systems do not use it.

The communitarian doubt about, and sometimes hostility to, takeovers is really another version of stakeholderism for it undermines property rights in exactly the same way. According to the stakeholder theory, the assets of an economy are not exclusively owned by individuals either directly or through institutions such as banks, insurance companies and investment funds. At most these institutions hold them in trust for the community. Therefore, individualistic striving for wealth should always be tempered and restrained by wider considerations. Some countries deliberately design laws which prevent valuable national assets, such as a long-established company, being taken over by foreigners. At the economic level the assumption is that the state knows better than the (global) market about investment opportunities, and at the moral level the claim is that there are values more important than individual want-satisfaction, even if they are not appreciated by transactors. The market might satisfy private interests but it consistently undervalues the public interest, and the communal goal is the public goal.[97]

But what is this communal, public or collective goal which is supposedly not captured by market capitalism? Although it is normally described as competitive, the market depends on certain common values, such as trust, honesty and respect for contract and property, which are not the result of the reasoning of a single designing mind, or even of the deliberations of many *via* a special contract. These values are the common inheritance of a civilisation or the shared legacy of a culture and are better preserved by the spontaneous and free development of a culture than by government action. That is why capitalism is consistent with a variety of social forms despite its reliance on a certain generic moral code.

Even under the most individualistic version of capitalism, certain common goods are recognised. For technical reasons the market cannot supply defence, clean air or law and order (though anarcho-capitalists demur) and we each have a common interest in their collective delivery. However, many of the alleged common goods cherished by communitarians favour one group at the expense of another. In the rejection of corporate reorganisation through the market, communitarians find themselves allying with the established group, threatened by the market, against the risk taking and innovative newcomer.

It is very easy for communitarians to press claims of public interest against the market because the criteria of what is in the public interest are so ambiguous, and its demands on transactors so diffuse, that the claims of any private group against the market can be admitted under its banner. The designers of British takeover regulations wisely inserted a provision in the Takeover Code that requires a proposed bid not to be *against* the public interest – by which they meant that it should not lead to monopoly or excessive market share – rather than that it should be *in* the public interest. If the latter were a requirement it could only generate disputes as to what the public interest really meant, and provide unlimited opportunities for sectional groups to claim that they had a better idea of the common good than an untrammelled market does. It is no surprise that political activists should campaign assiduously for the insertion of the more contentious interpretation of the public interest into the Takeover Code. If communities do have a precise understanding of common goods and a coherent set of beliefs that bind people, then the expansive notion of the public interest might be appropriate. However, in the pluralistic Anglo-American economic world such a demand can only be productive of more rivalry as each self-interested group presses its claims on the state.

TAKEOVERS IN NEW ZEALAND

Although as an Anglo-American type of economy New Zealand uses the familiar takeover method to police management (a role that banks play in some other economies) and to effect industrial reorganisation, there are significant differences in New Zealand law and practice. These differences arise largely from the peculiar features of the New Zealand stock market. The main features are its size (it is very small, comprising only around 0.2 percent of the world's capital market) and its composition (the market is characterised by significant concentrations, with around 80 percent of listed companies having a single block shareholder). This concentration of ownership can have good and bad features – it can lead to closer monitoring and greater participation of owners in management (helping to solve the agency problem) but it can also lead to unjust treatment of small shareholders who may be defenceless against large holders who own controlling shares. The latter problem is a general one, however, and it is not confined to the takeover situation.

The ethical debate about takeovers in New Zealand has been conducted almost exclusively at the micro level, that is, it is about the particular rules and practices that should govern transactions. All people who believe in the ethics of Anglo-American capitalism accept, in principle, that the takeover device is efficient (it encourages appropriate allocations of resources) and also just, since share ownership is a natural implication of property rights theory. Whatever regulation is in place, be it statute law or self-regulation by stock market rules, it should aim at making the takeover market more competitive. If the takeover market is competitive then the market for corporate control satisfies both efficiency and justice requirements. Research shows that, in common with other Anglo-American economies, shareholders in New Zealand have benefited from takeovers.[98] Even though critics still repeat the conventional mantras about paper shuffling and casino capitalism, it is clear that there have been genuine increases in ordinary shareholder wealth through takeovers. However, there have been continuing complaints about takeovers and the stock market in New Zealand. Share prices were slower to recover from the crash of 1987 than they were elsewhere, and there was even a naïve belief that the crash itself was partly a consequence of New Zealand's relatively lightly regulated regime.

Takeovers are often criticised because small shareholders do not necessarily get the same price from a takeover as large shareholders. Critics have found this offensive to equality and justice and have demanded reform. The issue arises because under New Zealand law and practice there is no requirement for a bidder to purchase the whole of the company (in British law, a bidder who captures 30 percent of a company in a takeover must make an offer for the rest) and different prices may be paid for the same class of shares. Therefore, there can be two-tier bids in which those who receive the first offer for their shares get more than those who come second. This is not allowed under the British Takeover Code, which requires that all shareholders be treated the same. However, these two restrictions are not a feature of federal securities law in the United States, although equal prices have to be paid in tender offers. Perhaps these ethical complaints have less resonance in the United States as takeovers tend to be highly contested and dispersed ownership means that successful bidders have to attract wide support – the equality principle tends to be automatically satisfied. A major objection to 'poison pills' is that they prevent a straight auction for the firm. An auction for a company is quite feasible in New Zealand although control can be transferred with only the major shareholder involved.

There have been attempts to make New Zealand takeover regulation more restrictive but the basic system – common law plus some statute law and an element of self-regulation – remains. In 1993, a Takeovers Panel, appointed under the Takeovers Act 1993, recommended a code which provoked intense economic and some ethical debate, but the code remained a dead letter.[99] Two of the most controversial recommendations were a 'mandatory offer' rule and an 'equal price' rule. The mandatory offer rule would have required an offer for all the shares if a 20 percent threshold (lower than the London Takeover Code) were reached; the equal price rule, by making one price obligatory for all, would have outlawed two-tier takeovers.

The rationale for the mandatory offer rule would appear to be that it was needed to stop self-dealing and the looting of small shareholders by large ones, although it was argued by the opponents of the code that this problem is a matter for company law and not takeover rules (the Companies Act 1993 went some way towards alleviating this problem by creating stricter fiduciary duties for directors). If the mandatory offer rule were ever to be adopted it could well reduce the number and the contestability of takeovers – having to make a full offer for the company might be very costly.[100] There is little evidence, however, that shareholders are dissatisfied, including overseas investors who have poured into New Zealand despite the absence of a heavy regulatory regime.

There is a good market justification for allowing different prices for the same type of share. In more closely held corporations, large shareholders can make a big contribution to the success of the firm by monitoring managements effectively. Small shareholders free ride on their efforts.[101] From an ethical viewpoint, why should minority shareholders share in a control premium they have not earned and have no reasonable expectation of earning? Even if small shareholders do not do as well as large ones in a takeover, they still gain from the activity. The implementation of the proposed 1993 code would have made takeovers more difficult, to everybody's cost. Furthermore, any limitation on the pricing of shares would involve an attenuation of property rights.

New Zealand publicly listed companies now have a choice of three different rules for takeovers, one of which is an equal treatment or 'minority veto' provision. Given this choice, it can be assumed that shareholders will choose the one that they believe will maximise shareholder value. In practice, few shareholders have chosen the more restrictive 'minority veto' option.[102]

Although takeovers in New Zealand are lightly regulated it cannot be said that the market is at variance with the rest of the Anglo-American business world. Such is the variety of regulatory regimes that it is difficult to say what the norm is. New Zealand is broadly in line with the United States, the world's leading securities market, in not having restrictive mandatory bid and equal price provisions.[103] Certainly the choices available in New Zealand mean that shareholders can adopt a more restrictive set of rules in line with the British practice, or they can choose more liberal ones. A mandatory bid and equal price rule, much favoured by moralists, can be adopted but it is not obligatory. The imposition of coercive, statutory law in this area would in fact be detrimental to efficiency and ethics.

5
BUSINESS ETHICS AND THE ENVIRONMENT

Investigation of the many concerns of contemporary business ethics shows that the question of property rights has been insufficiently explored by writers in the mainstream of the discipline. The harmful consequences of a lack of consideration of property rights are noticeable in at least two areas: where harm has been caused by market transactors and where the applicability of the many extra moral duties that are attributed to business affects people's legitimate holdings or assets. In both of these areas business moralists tend to invoke an abstract principle of moral philosophy (not of business practice) and make this part of a universally valid business ethic regardless of particular circumstances (thus equality requires positive discrimination in the workplace or no informational advantages to anyone in the stock market). Some of the disadvantages of this philosophy are treated as harms in need of correction or compensation irrespective of the rights of those who have to bear the cost, and the supererogatory duties are imposed with little or no consideration of the rights (normally of shareholders) that are then eroded. The implementation of these extra moral duties could have an adverse effect on the rights of owners, but business moralists do not regard ownership as being decisive; proprietors are expected to bear the costs of supererogatory duties and those costs necessitated by an expanded notion of harm.

However, it is in those aspects of business life, which should be morally appraised by the 'no harm' principle, that the property rights argument is most relevant, because the 'do nots' that ethics prescribes are almost always about violations of property rights (theft, fraud and deception being the obvious examples). Property rights arguments can also enter business ethics in more subtle ways. Where disputes about values might appear, superficially, to be intractable, the application of property rights arguments can have a dissolving effect. An example is the environment, where the translation of the case of a social wrong, such as unconscionable pollution, into a case of the violation of individual property rights might do something to calm the hysteria that surrounds environmental issues and to lessen the demands for collectivist solutions. The current emphasis on legislative and bureaucratic solutions to environmental problems poses a threat to business, in the utilitarian sense of reducing economic efficiency by making compliance costs too high, and also in a moral sense by depriving commercial agents of the fundamental right of exchange, or at least attenuating their rights.

THE ENVIRONMENTAL CRAZE

The word 'craze' is not used lightly, or without serious intent, because the reaction to many current problems of pollution, damage to the environment, depletion of species, so-called over-population and exhaustion of natural resources has often been a curious combination of sentimentality and irrational panic. This reaction has been coupled with a desire to persecute (morally and legally) the alleged perpetrators of environmental wrongs. The major, if not sole, victim of both excessive government control and ideological torment has been the business community. Businesses driven by self-interest and the profit motive are assumed to have no concern for the environment, and the capitalistic private property system is condemned outright for its supposed malefactions.

However, empirical evidence shows that the gravest environmental problems have occurred in countries with the least developed private property rights systems. Their governments' acclaimed purpose has been the elimination of market capitalism and the promotion of the 'public good' as opposed to selfish, private interests. Whole areas of Eastern Europe and Russia have been laid waste by the uncontrolled production of basically unwanted goods. The Aral Sea, a vast expanse of inland water, has been rendered virtually useless for anything productive by the effect of industrial pollution. However, governments that fall well short of communism have also not been great protectors of the environment.[104] New Zealand's record with fertiliser subsidies, land clearance schemes and the 'Think Big' projects is a case in point.

Elementary political economy tells us that if there is no price attached to anything it may be exploited. In socialist countries the environment has been plundered by governments as if it were a free resource. Even in so-called 'unregulated' capitalist countries, the value of a clean environment tends to rise as people's tastes for pleasant surroundings gradually takes priority over the production of goods and services, and this change in taste has had some beneficial effect on the environment. However, capitalist economies are not unregulated since private property rights are protected by law, and although the legal system has often not been allowed to develop in a way that would enable common environmental problems to be the subject of private action, it is along these lines that solutions should be sought. Private owners of businesses have the greatest incentives to protect valued resources. Even where there are genuine public good problems, and no incentive for each person separately to take preventive action, as in the celebrated 'tragedy of the commons' (where resources are unowned and get over-exploited), the solutions should embrace and redirect the motivations – primarily self-interest – that have been so successful in the production of conventional goods and services. A salubrious environment is a conventional good, the demand for which will be a function of people's tastes. The solution is to redesign the legal system so that there is a more accurate way of implementing people's subjective preferences for a clean environment, and a more efficient way of deterring those who would damage our common assets – clean air, fresh flowing waters and pleasant countryside.

Recommending a redesign of the legal system, clarifying property rights and pricing scarce resources is quite a different approach from that often adopted in the current environmental debate. Some protagonists for the environment have a very different project: the elevation of their preferences for a certain kind of environment and level of species preservation against any other conception. In its extreme forms this project would mean the end of economic growth. The capitalist market is rejected by advocates of this project because it offers the opportunity for a variety of preferences for different sorts of economic goals to be coordinated through the price system. For example, the United States is constantly castigated for consuming a vast amount of energy (and generating more carbon dioxide than any other country), but the welfare of its citizens is enhanced because it produces enormous supplies of goods and services and a reasonably pleasant environment. Socialist countries consume nearly as much energy for a fraction of America's productivity.

ENVIRONMENTALIST ETHICS

It is precisely this trade-off between competing human goals – economic growth and protection of the planet – that some environmentalists seek to end. For them, a free-market economic and environmental approach is redolent of 'instrumental reason', a limited conception of reason, deriving perhaps from David Hume, which regards our goals as being subjectively determined (none having priority over any other).[105] In this conception, reason is given the somewhat pedestrian task of calculating ways of achieving these goals, or pointing to possible incompatibilities between them.

For these environmentalists, however, reason has a more expansive and ambitious role. Its role is to adjudicate between our values and assign priorities with the purpose of preserving a clean environment and protecting every species against ruin by modern society, and in particular capitalists. There is no trade-off between competing human ends and no delicate cost-benefit analysis of alternative strategies to deal with perceived harms, but instead the complete submission of all human ends to the environmentalist ethic. This approach has much in common with religion, in that human needs are denied in favour of nature, but with one important proviso: the major religions of the world have regarded human society as being under a duty to tame nature, not lie down before it.

It might seem odd to say that the environment has rights in the way that humans (or even animals) do, but the arguments are conducted in terms that imply that it does. To put the interests of persons ahead of a rare species or environmental preservation is regarded as the egoistic demands of mere humankind, an example of 'speciesism'.

To the religious environmentalist, human needs are of no account when placed against the needs of the environment. An example of how this anti-human attitude creeps into public policy is the almost universal banning of insecticides. The elimination of DDT has led to a resurgence of malaria and a significant increase in deaths in countries such as Sri Lanka. However, the subordination of human ends to the demands of 'nature' is the major intent of the quasi-religious environmentalist; a number of avoidable deaths are of no consequence.

The trouble with the quasi-religious approach to the environment is that it discourages the use of evidence in the evaluation of problems. The religious aspect deliberately discounts the use of science. Even the global warming 'crisis', which has been presented as if it were capable of scientific resolution, has not been treated in a genuinely scientific way by the protagonists of excessive regulation and a slowdown in economic growth. The supposed excess of carbon dioxide in the atmosphere, which prevents natural cooling processes from operating effectively, is assumed to be the result of modern, capitalist production processes. However, it is now known that much of the temperature variation is a product of natural changes in the atmosphere, and in this context recent changes are relatively insignificant. [106] All this has been established by the use of sophisticated measuring devices and scientific models. The natural response of the environmentalist in the face of such evidence is to invoke the 'precautionary principle'; this tells us that although the adverse evidence may not be completely convincing, society ought to refrain from scientific and industrial progress in case it should turn out that way. If that principle had been decisive in the past there would not have been an industrial revolution and millions more would have been condemned to short, miserable lives.

Some of the more temperate environmental campaigners are prepared to give more weight to human needs in the consideration of environmental issues. Nevertheless, many seem to be convinced that a market subject only to the rule of law and well defined property rights cannot solve either the problem of damage to nature caused by industrialisation or the depletion of scarce resources. Their complaints raise an ethical question of intergenerational justice: the earth is not a resource which belongs exclusively to one generation but is a common property of humanity. However, the 'command and control' approach favoured by those environmentalists as a solution to these alleged problems is, implicitly if not explicitly, socialistic. It has a predilection for national plans, international targets and the deliberate direction of economic activity towards predetermined environmental goals. Like socialism's failure to produce ordinary goods and services, central planning of the environment founders on the *knowledge* problem. How can any central planner know people's preferences for economic growth over environmental protection (which will largely be a function of income)? How do blanket bans and confiscatory taxes capture special circumstances (it would be absurd to have the same laws about car pollution in Los Angeles *and* rural Montana)? Although some pollution problems are international, most are purely local, and some jurisdictional competition in environmental matters is to be welcomed as a method for the expression of preferences for economic efficiency over restrictive legislation and high taxation. Not all regulations and law would be driven down to the most permissive level in order to attract industry. People have various levels of preference for a clean environment, and their preferences are likely to get more intense beyond the early stages of industrialisation.

However, this incremental and evolutionary approach is distorted by an ethic that demands environmental 'justice' – that every person and every neighbourhood should have equality in the consumption of clean air, litter-free streets and pristine rural retreats. Environmentalists point out that poorer areas suffer most from environmental degradation: there are more landfills and smokey chimneys in such areas. There is, of course, a good economic reason for this: work that may be located in unpleasant environs is actually needed for employment and wealth creation that will, in turn, fuel the demand for more pleasant conditions. The demand for environmental justice, if successful, will lead to worse economic conditions for the poor.

Unfortunately, environmentalist arguments are increasingly put in the form of rights claims and this has had an unproductive effect on debate, because it removes from argument those subtleties and nuances that are intrinsically a part of the issue. Pollution is not always a bad; in fact it is difficult to imagine an economic process that doesn't have adverse effects on somebody. The problem, as we saw in chapter one, is the *extra* polluter who turns a socially productive process into one of overall disutility. Often the extra polluter cannot be identified. In a regime of completely specified property rights, some compromise would be reached between the claims of the environmentalist and the producer *via* the price system. However, in traditional political and moral theory the assertion of a right functions as an argument stopper: a rights possessor has an absolute claim which brooks no qualification that might derive from utility or even communitarianism. The compelling nature of rights claims derives from the traditional civil liberties, where it has a certain plausibility, and that is the tactical reason why it is used by environmentalists.

BUSINESS AND THE ENVIRONMENT

In a sense, business cannot win against the politically (and morally) active environmentalists in the argument over environmental issues since the latter are not normally interested in economics and in the necessary trade-offs that have to take place in a world of competing demands. Although they may talk of 'sustainable development', a suitably anodyne phrase that seems to give a place for the needs of humanity, this is not sufficiently precise to function as a guide to public policy. It would be better if business personnel could cooperate in environment-friendly commercial strategies but, as noted earlier, the tendency for any one agent to defect from a putative agreement in anonymous economies may be irresistible.[107] The clean air and clean water legislation in the United States has created tremendous compliance costs for business with little tangible benefit for the community, but one wonders how it could have been averted through voluntary restraint by business.

Environmental activists seek to work for a change in human nature to solve environmental problems. Agitators and pressure groups engage in constant campaigns to dissuade business from undertaking new developments. A large part of the not inconsiderable income of Greenpeace is spent on these activities.[108] Such activists do not invest in land purchase for environmental projects and do not conduct experiments in species preservation, as many free-market environmentalists do. They also engage in and encourage law breaking, as in the case of Greenpeace's long campaign against Royal Dutch/ Shell.[109] However, human nature is unchangeable and is governed by the same motivations as it always has been – for money, power and moral vanity (feeling good about yourself at little personal cost). As David Hume said, "... the utmost we can do is to change our circumstances and situation and render the observance of the laws of justice our nearest interest and their violation the most remote".[110] When motivational change fails to materialise, and moral blackmail does not have the required effect, inevitably environmental activists lobby for legislative coercion (the ground having already been softened by moral propaganda).

What is needed to protect the environment is not an environmental ethics but more emphasis on a sophisticated property rights system which 'internalises' the cost of damage. This does not mean simply the 'polluter pays' principle, for it often may be in doubt whose rights are violated. After all, does the resident have the right to silence or the airline the right to use jet engines? In the absence of transaction costs, according to economic theory, it does not matter how the property rights are distributed since a solution to an externality problem can always be reached by negotiation between the affected parties. If someone (or many people) feel badly about some environmental depredation they will buy out the perpetrator's rights. Of course, there may be significant transaction cost problems because large numbers of people may be difficult to organise (and there are potentially serious free-rider problems), but the property rights approach seems desirable wherever it is applicable, precisely because it economises on morality.

There is much evidence from legal history to show that some of the problems of the environment are solved by the common law in a case-by-case manner. A good example of this relates to water pollution in Britain today.[111] Anglers have for some time been taking legal action against polluters. Landowners have the riparian rights to the rivers that flow over their land and they sell licences to anglers who then acquire a legal right to sue for damages if an upstream polluter harms their fishing areas. In the United States similar common law remedies are more difficult to secure; there is proportionately less private ownership of rivers and, equally important, the Clean Water Act 1972 effectively rules out common law remedies. But before the law was enacted a number of important common law decisions went in favour of riparian owners. In one case, *Walden v Union Bag and Paper Co* [1913], an upstate New York paper mill discharged effluent that damaged a riparian owner's water.[112] The investment was quite significant and the damage was not great but the court, correctly, ruled that the firm should have found out whose rights were affected and negotiated a settlement. Here was a perfectly valid use of the word 'right' – it was a genuine claim arising out of common law and property rights – and in this case it nicely defeated utility. Similar solutions to environmental problems could emerge in a gradual, evolutionary manner. In this way people's rights are respected and preferences for the environment over prosperity can be registered. It is an efficient process which has been all but eliminated by statute in many countries.

Some improvement in statutory law has come about in a number of jurisdictions in the 1990s with the spread of pollution permits – up to a certain point producers can buy the right to pollute.[113] This gives producers an incentive to invest in pollution control devices and those who do not invest have to pay the cost of their own anti-social activity. Also, environmental enthusiasts may get together and buy up pollution permits. Some organisations can certainly afford to do this. The major difficulty with the scheme is that the actual levels of pollution to be permitted are determined by the government. Thus the approach is not properly subjectivist, and it reflects the questionable assumption that the government has some special insight into the appropriate level of pollution. The problem would be partially ameliorated if pollution decisions were taken at the lowest level of government.

However, use of the price mechanism can help to mitigate problems that are likely to become submerged in endless ethical argument. The same applies to the preservation of scarce resources. Here, the intuitive assumption that trade will threaten the existence of scarce resources is factually, and theoretically, false. The spread of commerce throughout the world over the past 30 years or so has actually helped to preserve certain so-called depletable resources. In 1970 economist Julian Simon made a famous bet with a well known doomsayer that 30 of the best known commodities (including oil) would be cheaper and more abundant in 10 years' time.[114] He won the bet.

The point is that market relationships constantly provide incentives for agents to improve production methods. As the price of a scarce good rises the search for close substitutes is stimulated. This process has been so successful of late that, as Simon predicted, prices have actually fallen. At one time there was a fear that elephants would become extinct because of trade in elephant tusks, and trade in tusks was therefore banned in many African countries. Yet in countries that allowed trade, mainly in southern Africa, elephant herds increased. This was because traders have a financial incentive to preserve the future value of the commodity. It yields an income over the long run, which is the only economic incentive that is required for conservation. In the case of scarce but renewable resources, more trade actually means more preservation.

CONCLUSION

As the example of the elephant herd shows, there is not necessarily a contradiction between economics and morality over environmental issues. However, many writers on business ethics assume that commerce has to be tamed by a sophisticated morality – that individualistic self-interest will not only threaten the delicate moral order on which civilised commerce depends, but the unrestrained market will also undermine the environment and civilisation itself. The critics neglect to notice that the market itself contains necessary rationing devices, mainly the system of pricing – the rarer the goods, the more they will cost – which ensures that value will be preserved. Only 'free' goods are wasted, and the reason why there is an environmental problem is that the common good takes on something of the nature of a free good. The solution is to establish property rights in the environment wherever possible. The rights will provide the necessary incentives to business to preserve clean air and water and pleasant amenities. It is partly an irrational hostility of critics to markets that prevents a wider spread of this technique.

In other areas of business, the assumption that self-interest corrodes our natural moral 'sensibilities' remains stubbornly entrenched. Leaving aside the question of whether there are any such sensibilities (it is just as plausible to suppose that moral behaviour is primarily a matter of learning the rules of just conduct), business is no more venal than other human activities just because the lure of private advantage seems more overt in it. In politics, greed and the lust for power are qualities that are just as prevalent, and politics lacks the benign governance of the 'invisible hand' to guide individual gratification in the direction of a modest common good.

Perhaps too much has been made of the differing types of capitalism. Although each may display a different type of institutional and financial superstructure, all types rest to a great extent on a generic moral code – which includes respect for justly acquired property; the sanctity of contract; the objective verdict of the market; (mainly) negative individual rights; and predictable, non-retrospective laws. Each transactor is not required to go beyond these constraints, and if they do so *voluntarily*, that action is worthy of respect. Such respect is much more deserved than if the transactor's action is the result of the moral pressure, if not blackmail, that is so often a feature of business ethics.

ENDNOTES

CHAPTER I

1   Michael Bassett, *The State in New Zealand 1840–1984: Socialism Without Doctrines?*, Auckland University Press, Auckland, 1998.

2   This began mainly in America, but has spread rapidly to Britain and Europe. Important introductory books are T Beauchamp and N Bowie (eds), *Ethical Theory and Business*, 4th edn, Prentice Hall, Englewood Cliffs, 1993; Elaine Sternberg, *Just Business*, Little Brown, London, 1994; T Sorell and J Hendry, *Business Ethics*, Butterworth-Heinemann, Oxford, 1994; N Barry, *Business Ethics*, Macmillan, London, 1998.

3   James D Gwartney and Robert A Lawson, *Economic Freedom of the World Report 1998*, Fraser Institute and others, Vancouver, 1998.

4   Roger Kerr, 'Markets and Morality: A Look at the Facts', *New Zealand Herald*, 26 September, 1996. There has been a lively debate in the press in New Zealand on the issue of the moral responsibility of business. See, for example, Nick Park, 'Business must be both responsible and moral', *The Independent*, 17 January, 1997.

5   *Sunday Star Times*, 1 February, 1998.

6   Adam Smith, *The Wealth of Nations*, R H Campbell and A S Skinner (eds), Clarenden Press, Oxford, 1970, pp 26–27.

7   Marjorie Grice-Hutchinson, *The School of Salamanca*, Oxford University Press, London, 1952.

8   Imad-ad-Dean Ahmad, 'Islam and Hayek', *Economic Affairs*, April, 1993.

9   However, many Catholics, particularly in South America, have adapted something close to Marxism to their religious creed.

10 The supply of public goods is always thwarted by the 'free rider' problem.

11 B Mandeville, *The Fable of the Bees*, F B Kaye (ed), Oxford University Press, London, 1924, first published in 1705, Vol 1, p 46.

12 *ibid*, p 369.

13 Quoted in R Reidenbach and D Robin, *Ethics and Profits*, Prentice Hall, Englewood Cliffs, 1989.

14 F Fukuyama, *Trust: The Social Virtues and the Creation of Prosperity*, Hamish Hamilton, London, 1995, pp 269–321.

15 D Hume, *A Treatise of Human Nature*, H Akin (ed), Macmillan, New York, 1948, first published 1740, Book III, p 612.

16 D Boaz, *Libertarianism: A Primer*, Free Press, New York, 1997.

17 W Röpke, *A Humane Economy*, Wolff, London, 1960, p 125.

18 This complex system is especially effective in preventing takeovers. See I Hiroyuki, 'The Banking-Industrial Complex', in D Okimoto and T Roblen (eds), *Inside the Japanese System*, Stanford University Press, Stanford, 1988.

19 N Barry, *Business Ethics*, *op cit*, pp 33–36.

20 For deontological ethics as applied to business, see *ibid*, ch 2.

CHAPTER 2

21 For the 'criminalisation' of the corporation, see N Barry, *The Morality of Business Enterprise*, Aberdeen University Press, David Hume Institute, Aberdeen, 1991, ch 2.

22 J K Galbraith, *American Capitalism: The Concept of Countervailing Power*, Houghton Mifflin, Boston, 1952.

23 D Robertson and S Dennison, *The Control of Industry*, Cambridge University Press, Cambridge, 1960, p 73.

24 R H Coase, 'The Nature of the Firm', *Economica*, 4, 1937, pp 386–405.

25 J Kuhn and D Shriver, *Beyond Success: Corporations and their Critics in the 1990s*, Oxford University Press, New York, 1991.

26 Robert Reich, reported in *Reason*, July 1996.

27 R Hessen, *In Defense of the Corporation*, Hoover Institution, Stanford, 1979, p 43.

28 *ibid*, chs 1–3.

29 Adrienne von Tunzelmann, *Social Responsibility and the Company: A New Perspective on Governance and the Community*, Institute of Policy Studies, Wellington, 1996, p 65.

30 Royal Society for Arts, Manufacturers and Commerce, London, 1995.

31 M R Griffiths and J R Lucas, *Ethical Economics*, Macmillan, London, 1996, pp 64–65.

32 N Barry, 'Liberty and Justice in Marriage and Divorce', in R Whelan (ed), *Just a Piece of Paper?*, Institute of Economic Affairs, London, 1996.

33 Marianne Curphey, 'Body Shop Stays in Public Ownership', *The Times*, 5 March, 1996.

34 M Friedman, 'The Social Responsibility of Business is to Increase its Profits', in Beauchamp and Bowie, *Ethical Theory and Business*, *op cit*, p 56 (see footnote 2).

35 Elaine Sternberg, *op cit*, p 41 (see footnote 2).

36 J Joseph, *No Man Can Serve Two Masters: Shareholders Versus Stakeholders in the Governance of Companies*, Social Affairs Unit, London, 1998, pp 5–6.

37 Von Tunzelmann, *op cit*, p ix (see footnote 29).

38 *ibid*, p 5.

39 N Barry, *Business Ethics*, *op cit*, pp 74–84 (see footnote 2).

40 In what was originally a hostile bid by Krupp for Thyssen to create a giant steel combine, trade unions, banks and community groups formed an alliance to convert the endeavour into a friendly (and tame) merger. See *The Economist*, 29 March, 1997.

41 W Evan and R Freeman, 'A Stakeholder Theory of the Modern Corporation', in Beauchamp and Bowie, *Ethical Theory and Business*, *op cit*, p 82 (see footnote 2).

42 M Keeley, *A Social Contract Theory of Organizations*, University of Notre Dame Press, Indiana, 1988.

43   Robert Reich, reported in *Reason*, July, 1996.

44   Reported in *The Press*, 28 August, 1998.

45   H Manne, *The Modern Corporation and Social Responsibility*, American Enterprise Institute, Washington DC, 1972, p 29.

46   The phrase is from Frederic Bastiat, the great French nineteenth century free-market economist. See D Boaz (ed), *Libertarianism: A Primer*, *op cit*, pp 265–273 (see footnote 16).

47   Nomura has been the subject of continuing investigation and legal action over the last few years. See *Financial Times*, 20 January, 1998.

48   The Bank of Credit and Commerce International offered very favourable interest rates to mainly Asian immigrants in Britain but was shot through with corruption and crime.

49   'Air Wars', *Financial Times*, 9 July, 1996.

50   Sir Adrian Cadbury, 'The Role of Voluntary Codes of Practice in Setting Ethics', in I Jones and M Pollitt (eds), *The Role of Business Ethics in Economic Performance*, University of Cambridge Press, Cambridge, 1998, p 76.

51   *Mens rea* is the requirement of a 'guilty mind' for a successful criminal prosecution.

52   *Code of Best Practice*, Gee Publishing, London, 1992. This is the report of the Committee on the Financial Aspects of Corporate Governance (Cadbury Report).

53   Cadbury, 'The Role of Voluntary Codes of Practice in Setting Ethics', *op cit*, p 83 (see footnote 50).

54   A O'Brien, 'Regulating Virtue: Engendering and Enforcing Codes of Ethics', in K Wolderung (ed), *Business Ethics in Australia and New Zealand*, Nelson, Melbourne, 1996.

55   *Report of the Wine-box Inquiry: Commission of Inquiry into Certain Matters Relating to Taxation*, GP Publications, Wellington, 1997.

56   The Employment Contracts Act 1991 abolished the prevailing central wage-fixing system based on compulsory and registered unions and national awards and allowed anyone to enter an individual or collective employment contract.

CHAPTER 3

57   N Barry, *Insider Dealing: An Exploration into Law and Existing Practice*, Foundation for Business Responsibilities, London, 1996.

58   Milken's final six-count indictment, to which he was subjected to great pressure to plead, did not include insider dealing charges, though they were on the original 98-count indictment.

59   H MacQueen (ed), *Insider Dealing*, David Hume Institute, Edinburgh, 1993.

60   Digby Anderson (ed), *What is Ethical about Ethical Investment?*, Social Affairs Unit, London, 1997.

61   'Insider Trading and the Law Professors', *Vanderbilt Law Review*, 23, 1970, p 549.

62   The 'robber barons' were the legendary industrialists who were accused of all sorts of nefarious practices in the consolidation of oil, coal, rail and utilities in the last century. They are receiving a slightly better press, even from the left, these days ('at least they produced something, they didn't just shuffle paper').

63   N Barry, *The Morality of Business Enterprise, op cit*, p 52 (see footnote 21).

64   Regulations issued under the Securities and Exchange Act 1934 allow considerable discretion to prosecuting authorities.

65   A Brennan and N Kubasek, *The Legal Environment of Business*, Macmillan, New York, 1988, pp 300–301.

66   *ibid*, p 301.

67   In the *Winans* case, a *Wall Street Journal* reporter had his conviction upheld for insider dealing: he had merely traded on his share tips, based on no inside information at all. See N Barry, *Business Ethics, op cit*, p 97 (see footnote 2).

68   The events are graphically described in D Frantz, *Levine and Co*, Holt, New York, 1987.

69   *Daily Telegraph*, 31 May, 1991.

70   B Hannigan, *Insider Dealing*, Kluwer, London, 1988, p 24.

71   Richard A Epstein, *The Concealment, Use and Disclosure of Information*, New Zealand Business Roundtable, Wellington, 1996, p 17.

72   *Percival v Wright* [1902]. See Hannigan, *Insider Dealing, op cit*, pp 23–25 (see footnote 70).

73   The economic case for unregulated insider dealing is made in H Manne, *Insider Trading and the Stock Market*, Free Press, New York, 1966.

74   *ibid*, p 8.

75   A Brown, 'Insider Dealing and the Criminal Law', in H MacQueen, *Insider Dealing, op cit*, pp 1–18 (see footnote 59).

76   N Barry, *Business Ethics, op cit*, p 112 (see footnote 2).

77   Mike Ross, 'Insider trading rules seldom get the real villains of the piece', *National Business Review*, 20 August, 1996.

78   Described critically in Roger Partridge, 'Our insider trading laws imperil the honest and unwary', *The Independent*, 11 March, 1998.

79   'Courts struggle with insider trading law', *The Independent*, 18 March, 1998.

CHAPTER 4

80   There was proportionately more takeover activity in the United States at the turn of the century than in the 1980s. See A T Peacock and G Bannock, *Corporate Takeovers and the Public Interest*, David Hume Institute, Edinburgh, 1991, ch 1.

81   Michael Jensen, 'Takeovers: Their Causes and Consequences', *Journal of Economic Perspectives*, Vol 2, No 1, 1988, pp 21–48.

82   A T Peacock and G Bannock, *op cit*, ch 4 (see footnote 80).

83   Michael Jensen, *op cit*, pp 23–25 (see footnote 81).

84   Amnon Mandelbaum, *Submission to the Takeovers Panel Advisory Committee on the Draft Takeovers Code*, New Zealand Business Roundtable, Wellington, 1993, pp 10–17.

85   For a brief account of Austrian economics, see N Barry, 'Austrian Economics: A Dissent from Orthodoxy', in D Greenaway *et al*, *A Companion to Contemporary Economic Thought*, Routledge, London, 1991.

86   Israel Kirzner, *Competition and Entrepreneurship*, University of Chicago Press, Chicago, 1973; and *Discovery, Capitalism and Distributive Justice*, Blackwell, Oxford, 1989. For an application of Kirzner's theory to takeovers, see N Barry, *Business Ethics, op cit*, ch 6 (see footnote 2).

87   Kirzner, *Discovery, Capitalism and Distributive Justice, ibid*, p 172.

88   F Modigliani and M Miller, 'The Cost of Capital, Corporate Finance, and the Theory of Investment', *American Economic Review*, 48, 1958, pp 261–297.

89   Saunders and his fellow conspirators were given five-year jail sentences.

90   M Ricketts, 'Kirzner's Theory of Entrepreneurship', in B Caldwell and S Bohm (eds), *Austrian Economics: Tensions and New Directions*, Kluwer, London, 1994, pp 80–81.

91   D Fischel, *Payback*, Harper, New York, 1995; also Barry, *The Morality of Business Enterprise, op cit*, (see footnote 21).

92   Milken actually got the idea from an obscure publication by W Bradford Hickman, *Corporate Bond Quality and Investor Experience*, source and date unknown.

93   R Sobel, *Dangerous Dreamers*, Wiley, New York, 1993.

94   For the business decision rule, see Jensen, *op cit*, p 42–44 (see footnote 81).

95   For the latest legal developments, see Barry, *Business Ethics, op cit*, p 134 (see footnote 2).

96   For an account of philosophical communitarianism, see S Mulhall and A Swift, *Liberals and Communitarians*, Blackwell, Oxford, 1992.

97   A Etzioni, *The Spirit of Community*, Crown, New York, 1993.

98   P Fitzsimons, 'New Zealand's Takeovers Regulation: the Unresolved Debate', *Agenda*, 1996, pp 317–326; John Pound (in collaboration with Richard J Zeckhauser), *The Market for Corporate Control*, New Zealand Centre for Independent Studies Occasional Paper, May, 1988.

99   See Mandelbaum, *op cit*, pp 18–26 (see footnote 84).

100 Fitzsimons, *op cit*, pp 318–325 (see footnote 98).

101 Mandelbaum, *op cit*, p 25 (see footnote 84).

102 See the New Zealand Business Roundtable's analysis of the 1995 Takeovers Panel Report, Wellington, 1995, p 11; Mandelbaum, *op cit*, pp 19–20 (see footnote 84).

103 As noted, in the United States equal prices have to be paid in tender offers.

CHAPTER 5

104 J Shaw, 'Environmental Dangers', in *PERC Resource Book on Pollution, Trade and Aid*, Political Economy Research Center, Montana, 1991.

105 M Bookchin, *The Ecology of Freedom: The Emergence and Dissolution of Hierarchy*, Cheshire, Palo Alto, 1989.

106 R Bate, 'Global Warning: Don't Believe All the Hype', *Wall Street Journal*, 11 December, 1995.

107 R Stroup, 'Property Rights, Justice and Efficient Environmental Policy', *Journal des Economistes et des Etudes Humaines*, 1997, pp 221–226.

108 M Ridley, *Down to Earth*, Institute of Economic Affairs, London, 1996.

109 *ibid*, ch 1.

110 D Hume, *A Treatise of Human Nature*, Fontana, London, 1972, first published in 1740, Book 3, p 220.

111 R Bate, 'Water Pollution Prevention: A Nuisance Approach', *Economic Affairs*, Vol 14, No 3, 1994, pp 13–14.

112 Barry, *Business Ethics, op cit*, p 165 (see footnote 2).

113 Barry, *ibid*, pp 165–166.

114 Reported in *Progressive Environmentalism*, National Center for Policy Analysis, Dallas, 1991.

INDEX